Level 1

¡Avancemos!

Unit 6 Resource Book

HOLT McDOUGAL
a division of Houghton Mifflin Harcourt

Fine Art Acknowledgments

Page 86 *Muchacho con cachucha* (1958), Jaime Colson. Tinta sobre papel, 32 cm x 25 cm.
Colección Museo Bellapart, Santo Domingo, República Dominicana.

Page 87 *Una madre*, Cándido Bidó. Acrylic, 40″ x 50″. Courtesy of Cándido Bidó Galería De Arte.

Page 88 *Sin título* (1960), Clara Ledesma. Oleo sobre línea, 135 cm x 198 cm. Colección Museo
Bellapart, Santo Domingo, República Dominicana.

Page 89 *Paisaje de lluvia* (1940), Darío Suro. Oleo/tela, 20″ x 28.5″. Courtesy of Colección
Museo Bellapart, Santo Domingo, República Dominicana.

ISBN-13: 978-0-618-76617-8
ISBN-10: 0-618-76617-0   12 13 14 1689 17 16 15
4500531933
Internet: www.holtmcdougal.com

HOLT McDOUGAL

¡Avancemos!

Table of Contents

To the Teacher

Welcome to *¡Avancemos!* This exciting new Spanish program from McDougal Littell has been designed to provide you—the teacher of today's foreign language classroom—with comprehensive pedagogical support.

PRACTICE WITH A PURPOSE

Activities throughout the program begin by establishing clear goals. Look for the **¡Avanza!** arrow that uses student-friendly language to lead the way towards achievable goals. Built-in self-checks in the student text (**Para y piensa:** Did you get it?) offer the chance to assess student progress throughout the lesson. Both the student text and the workbooks offer abundant leveled practice to match varied student needs.

CULTURE AS A CORNERSTONE

¡Avancemos! celebrates the cultural diversity of the Spanish-speaking world by motivating students to think about similarities and contrasts among different Spanish-speaking cultures. Essential questions encourage thoughtful discussion and comparison between different cultures.

LANGUAGE LEARNING THAT LASTS

The program presents topics in manageable chunks that students will be able to retain and recall. "Recycle" topics are presented frequently so students don't forget material from previous lessons. Previously learned content is built upon and reinforced across the different levels of the program.

TIME-SAVING TEACHER TOOLS

Simplify your planning with McDougal Littell's exclusive teacher resources: the all-inclusive EasyPlanner DVD-ROM, ready-made Power Presentations, and the McDougal Littell Assessment System.

Unit Resource Book

Each Unit Resource Book supports a unit of *¡Avancemos!* The Unit Resource Books provide a wide variety of materials to support, practice, and expand on the material in the *¡Avancemos!* student text.

Components **Following is a list of components included in each Unit Resource Book:**

BACK TO SCHOOL RESOURCES (UNIT 1 ONLY)

Review and start-up activities to support the **Lección preliminar** of the textbook.

DID YOU GET IT? RETEACHING & PRACTICE COPYMASTERS

If students' performance on the **Para y piensa** self-check for a section does not meet your expectations, consider assigning the corresponding Did You Get It? Reteaching and Practice Copymasters. These copymasters provide extensive reteaching and additional practice for every vocabulary and grammar presentation section in *¡Avancemos!* Each vocabulary and grammar section has a corresponding three-page copymaster. The first page of the copymaster reteaches the subject material in a fresh manner. Immediately following this presentation page are two pages of practice exercises that help the student master the topic. The practice pages have engaging contexts and structures to retain students' attention.

PRACTICE GAMES

These games provide fun practice of the vocabulary and grammar just taught. They are targeted in scope so that each game practices a specific area of the **lesson**: *Práctica de vocabulario*, *Vocabulario en contexto*, *Práctica de gramática*, *Gramática en contexto*, *Todo junto*, *Repaso de la lección*, and the lesson's cultural information.

Video and audio resources

VIDEO ACTIVITIES

These two-page copymasters accompany the Vocabulary Video and each scene of the **Telehistoria** in Levels 1 and 2 and the **Gran desafío** in Level 3. The pre-viewing activity asks students to activate prior knowledge about a theme or subject related to the scene they will watch. The viewing activity is a simple activity for students to complete as they watch the video. The post-viewing activity gives students the opportunity to demonstrate comprehension of the video episode.

VIDEO SCRIPTS

This section provides the scripts of each video feature in the unit.

AUDIO SCRIPTS

This section contains scripts for all presentations and activities that have accompanying audio in the student text as well as in the two workbooks (*Cuaderno: práctica por niveles* and *Cuaderno para hispanohablantes*) and the assessment program.

Culture resources

MAP/CULTURE ACTIVITIES

This section contains a copymaster with geography and culture activities based on the Unit Opener in the textbook.

FINE ART ACTIVITIES

The fine art activities in every lesson ask students to analyze pieces of art that have been selected as representative of the unit location country. These copymasters can be used in conjunction with the full-color fine art transparencies in the Unit Transparency Book.

Home-school connection

FAMILY LETTERS & FAMILY INVOLVEMENT ACTIVITIES

This section is designed to help increase family support of the students' study of Spanish. The family letter keeps families abreast of the class's progress, while the family involvement activities let students share their Spanish language skills with their families in the context of a game or fun activity.

ABSENT STUDENT COPYMASTERS

The Absent Student Copymasters enable students who miss part of a **lesson** to go over the material on their own. The checkbox format allows teachers to choose and indicate exactly what material the student should complete. The Absent Student Copymasters also offer strategies and techniques to help students understand new or challenging information.

Core Ancillaries in the ¡Avancemos! Program

Leveled workbooks

CUADERNO: PRÁCTICA POR NIVELES

This core ancillary is a leveled practice workbook to supplement the student text. It is designed for use in the classroom or as homework. Students who can complete the activities correctly should be able to pass the quizzes and tests. Practice is organized into three levels of difficulty, labeled A, B, and C. Level B activities are designed to practice vocabulary, grammar, and other core concepts at a level appropriate to most of your students. Students who require more structure can complete Level A activities, while students needing more of a challenge should be encouraged to complete the activities in Level C. Each level provides a different degree of linguistic support, yet requires students to know and handle the same vocabulary and grammar content.

The following sections are included in *Cuaderno: práctica por niveles* for each **lesson**:

Vocabulario A, B, C	Escuchar A, B, C
Gramática 1 A, B, C	Leer A, B, C
Gramática 2 A, B, C	Escribir A, B, C
Integración: Hablar	Cultura A, B, C
Integración: Escribir	

CUADERNO PARA HISPANOHABLANTES

This core ancillary provides leveled practice for heritage learners of Spanish. Level A is for heritage learners who hear Spanish at home but who may speak little Spanish themselves. Level B is for those who speak some Spanish but don't read or write it yet and who may lack formal education in Spanish. Level C is for heritage learners who have had some formal schooling in Spanish. These learners can read and speak Spanish, but may need further development of their writing skills. The *Cuaderno para hispanohablantes* will ensure that heritage learners practice the same basic grammar, reading, and writing skills taught in the student text. At the same time, it offers additional instruction and challenging practice designed specifically for students with prior knowledge of Spanish.

The following sections are included in *Cuaderno para hispanohablantes* for each **lesson**:

Vocabulario A, B, C	Integración: Hablar
Vocabulario adicional	Integración: Escribir
Gramática 1 A, B, C	Lectura A, B, C
Gramática 2 A, B, C	Escritura A, B, C
Gramática adicional	Cultura A, B, C

ASSESSMENT PROGRAM

For each level of *¡Avancemos!*, there are four complete assessment options. Every option assesses students' ability to use the lesson and unit vocabulary and grammar, as well as assessing reading, writing, listening, speaking, and cultural knowledge. The on-level tests are designed to assess the language skills of most of your students. Modified tests provide more support, explanation and scaffolding to enable students with learning difficulties to produce language at the same level as their peers. Pre-AP* tests build the test-taking skills essential to success on Advanced Placement tests. The assessments for heritage learners are all in Spanish, and take into account the strengths that native speakers bring to language learning.

In addition to leveled lesson and unit tests, there is a complete array of vocabulary, culture, and grammar quizzes. All tests include scoring rubrics and point teachers to specific resources for remediation.

UNIT TRANSPARENCY BOOKS—1 PER UNIT

Each transparency book includes:

- Map Atlas Transparencies (Unit 1 only)
- Unit Opener Map Transparencies
- Fine Art Transparencies
- Vocabulary Transparencies
- Grammar Presentation Transparencies
- Situational Transparencies with Label Overlay (plus student copymasters)
- Warm Up Transparencies
- Student Book and Workbook Answer Transparencies

LECTURAS PARA TODOS

A workbook-style reader, *Lecturas para todos*, offers all the readings from the student text as well as additional literary readings in an interactive format. In addition to the readings, they contain reading strategies, comprehension questions, and tools for developing vocabulary.

There are four sections in each *Lecturas para todos*:

- *¡Avancemos!* readings with annotated skill-building support
- *Literatura adicional*—additional literary readings
- Academic and Informational Reading Development
- Test Preparation Strategies

* AP and the Advanced Placement Program are registered trademarks of the College Entrance Examination Board, which was not involved in the production of and does not endorse this product.

LECTURAS PARA HISPANOHABLANTES

Lecturas para hispanohablantes offers additional cultural readings for heritage learners and a rich selection of literary readings. All readings are supported by reading strategies, comprehension questions, tools for developing vocabulary, plus tools for literary analysis.

There are four sections in each *Lecturas para hispanohablantes*:

- *En voces* cultural readings with annotated skill-building support
- *Literatura adicional*—high-interest readings by prominent authors from around the Spanish-speaking world. Selections were chosen carefully to reflect the diversity of experiences Spanish-speakers bring to the classroom.
- Bilingual Academic and Informational Reading Development
- Bilingual Test Preparation Strategies, for success on standardized tests in English

COMIC BOOKS

These fun, motivating comic books are written in a contemporary, youthful style with full-color illustrations. Each comic uses the target language students are learning. There is one 32-page comic book for each level of the program.

TPRS: TEACHING PROFICIENCY THROUGH READING AND STORYTELLING

This book includes an up-to-date guide to TPRS and TPRS stories written by Piedad Gutiérrez that use *¡Avancemos!* lesson-specific vocabulary.

MIDDLE SCHOOL RESOURCE BOOK

- Practice activities to support the 1b Bridge lesson
- Diagnostic and Bridge Unit Tests
- Transparencies
  - Vocabulary Transparencies
  - Grammar Transparencies
  - Answer Transparencies for the Student Text
  - Bridge Warm Up Transparencies
- Audio CDs

LESSON PLANS

- Lesson Plans with suggestions for modifying instruction
- Core and Expansion options clearly noted
- IEP suggested modifications
- Substitute teacher lesson plans

BEST PRACTICES TOOLKIT

Strategies for Effective Teaching

- Research-based Learning Strategies
- Language Learning that Lasts: Teaching for Long-term Retention
- Culture as a Cornerstone/Cultural Comparisons
- English Grammar Connection
- Building Vocabulary
- Developing Reading Skills
- Differentiation
- Best Practices in Teaching Heritage Learners
- Assessment (including Portfolio Assessment, Reteaching and Remediation)
- Best Practices Swap Shop: Favorite Activities for Teaching Reading, Writing, Listening, Speaking
- Reading, Writing, Listening, and Speaking Strategies in the World Languages classroom
- ACTFL Professional Development Articles
- Thematic Teaching
- Best Practices in Middle School

Using Technology in the World Languages Classroom

Tools for Motivation

- Games in the World Languages Classroom
- Teaching Proficiency through Reading and Storytelling
- Using Comic Books for Motivation

Pre-AP and International Baccalaureate

- International Baccalaureate
- Pre-AP

Graphic Organizer Transparencies

- Teaching for Long-term Retention
- Teaching Culture
- Building Vocabulary
- Developing Reading Skills

Absent Student Copymasters—Tips for Students

LISTENING TO CDS AT HOME

- Open your text, workbook, or class notes to the corresponding pages that relate to the audio you will listen to. Read the assignment directions if there are any. Do these steps before listening to the audio selections.

- Listen to the CD in a quiet place. Play the CD loudly enough so that you can hear everything clearly. Keep focused. Play a section several times until you understand it. Listen carefully. Repeat aloud with the CD. Try to sound like the people on the CD. Stop the CD when you need to do so.

- If you are lost, stop the CD. Replay it and look at your notes. Take a break if you are not focusing. Return and continue after a break. Work in short periods of time: 5 or 10 minutes at a time so that you remain focused and energized.

QUESTION/ANSWER SELECTIONS

- If there is a question/answer selection, read the question aloud several times. Write down the question. Highlight the key words, verb endings, and any new words. Look up new words and write their meaning. Then say everything aloud.

- One useful strategy for figuring out questions is to put parentheses around groups of words that go together. For example: **(¿Cuántos niños)(van)(al estadio)(a las tres?)** Read each group of words one at a time. Check for meaning. Write out answers. Highlight key words and verb endings. Say the question aloud. Read the answer aloud. Ask yourself if you wrote what you meant.

- Be sure to say everything aloud several times before moving on to the next question. Check for spelling, verb endings, and accent marks.

FLASHCARDS FOR VOCABULARY

- If you have Internet access, go to ClassZone at classzone.com. All the vocabulary taught in *¡Avancemos!* is available on electronic flashcards. Look for the flashcards in the *¡Avancemos!* section of ClassZone.

- If you don't have Internet access, write the Spanish word or phrase on one side of a 3″ × 5″ card, and the English translation on the other side. Illustrate your flashcards when possible. Be sure to highlight any verb endings, accent marks, or other special spellings that will need a bit of extra attention.

GRAMMAR ACTIVITIES

- Underline or highlight all verb endings and adjective agreements. For example: **Nosotros comemos pollo rico.**

- Underline or highlight infinitive endings: **trabajar**.

- Underline or highlight accented letters. Say aloud and be louder on the accented letters. Listen carefully for the loudness. This will remind you where to write your accent mark. For example: **lápiz**, **lápices**, **árbol**, **árboles**

- When writing a sentence, be sure to ask yourself, "What do I mean? What am I trying to say?" Then check your sentence to be sure that you wrote what you wanted to say.

- Mark patterns with a highlighter. For example, for stem-changing verbs, you can draw a "boot" around the letters that change:

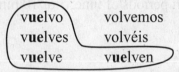

READING AND CULTURE SECTIONS

- Read the strategy box. Copy the graphic organizer so you can fill it out as you read.

- Look at the title and subtitles before you begin to read. Then look at and study any photos and read the captions. Translate the captions only if you can't understand them at all. Before you begin to read, guess what the selection will be about. What do you think that you will learn? What do you already know about this topic?

- Read any comprehension questions before beginning to read the paragraphs. This will help you focus on the upcoming reading selection. Copy the questions and highlight key words.

- Reread one or two of the questions and then go to the text. Begin to read the selection carefully. Read it again. On a sticky note, write down the appropriate question number next to where the answer lies in the text. This will help you keep track of what the questions have asked you and will help you focus when you go back to reread it later, perhaps in preparation for a quiz or test.

- Highlight any new words. Make a list or flashcards of new words. Look up their meanings. Study them. Quiz yourself or have a partner quiz you. Then go back to the comprehension questions and check your answers from memory. Look back at the text if you need to verify your answers.

PAIRED PRACTICE EXERCISES

- If there is an exercise for partners, practice both parts at home.

- If no partner is available, write out both scripts and practice both roles aloud. Highlight and underline key words, verb endings, and accent marks.

WRITING PROJECTS

- Brainstorm ideas before writing.

- Make lists of your ideas.

- Put numbers next to the ideas to determine the order in which you want to write about them.

- Group your ideas into paragraphs.

- Skip lines in your rough draft.

- Have a partner read your work and give you feedback on the meaning and language structure.

- Set it aside and reread it at least once before doing a final draft. Double-check verb endings, adjective agreements, and accents.

- Read it once again to check that you said what you meant to say.

- Be sure to have a title and any necessary illustrations or bibliography.

Did You Get It? *Presentación de vocabulario*

> **¡AVANZA!**   **Goal:**   Learn the words to talk about sports.

Sports

- Different sports require different equipment for players **(los jugadores)**, and different places for playing. Study the chart below.

Sports	Equipment Needed	Where Played
el básquetbol *(basketball)*	**la pelota** *(ball)*	**la cancha** *(court)*
el béisbol *(baseball)*	**el bate** *(bat)* **el casco** *(helmet)* **el guante** *(glove)* **la pelota** *(ball)*	**el campo** *(field)*
el fútbol americano *(football)*	**la pelota** *(ball)* **el casco** *(helmet)*	**el campo** *(field)* **el estadio** *(stadium)*
la natación *(swimming)*	**el traje de baño** *(swimsuit)*	**la piscina** *(pool)*
patinaje en línea *(inline skating)*	**los patines en línea** *(inline skates)*	
el tenis *(tennis)*	**la pelota** *(ball)* **la raqueta** *(racket)*	**la cancha** *(court)*
el voleibol *(volleyball)*	**la pelota** *(ball)*	**la cancha** *(court)*

- There are other words and expressions you can use to talk about sports. Learn some of these words in the paragraph below.

    There are two ways to enjoy *sports* **(los deportes)**. One is to be *a player* **(un jugador)**; the other is to be a spectator, or fan. Fans, or **aficionados**, as they are called in both Spanish and English, *understand the rules of the game well* **(comprenden bien las reglas del partido)**. Some sports can be more *dangerous* **(peligrosos)** than others. All *athletes* **(atletas)**, not just *champions* **(los campeones)**, play to *to win* **(ganar)**. Do you have *favorite sport* **(un deporte favorito)**? Do you play on *team* **(un equipo)**? Do you like *to lose* **(perder)**?

Did You Get It? *Práctica de vocabulario*

¡AVANZA! **Goal:** Learn the words to talk about sports.

❶ Which do you need for . . .

1. baseball?

los patines en línea   la raqueta   el bate

2. tennis?

el guante   la raqueta   el casco

3. football?

el casco   el bate   el guante

4. basketball?

la pelota   los patines en línea   la raqueta

5. inline skating?

los patines en línea   la raqueta   el guante

❷ Where is each sport played?

la cancha	el campo	la piscina	el estadio

1. el básquetbol _____   **4.** el tenis _____

2. el béisbol _____   **5.** el voleibol _____

3. la natación _____   **6.** el fútbol _____

❸ What sport and equipment are shown in each picture?

1.   2.   3.   4.   5.

1. _____

2. _____

3. _____

4. _____

5. _____

4 Translate the italicized words and phrases into Spanish.

jugadora	aficionados	cascos	raqueta	perder
las reglas	atleta	peligroso	guante	ganar

1. Es importante comprender *the rules* del partido. _____

2. Somos *fans* del fútbol. _____

3. Es divertido *to win* un partido. _____

4. No me gusta *to lose*. _____

5. Dolores es una buena *athlete*. _____

6. Es la mejor *player* del equipo. _____

7. El fútbol americano puede ser *dangerous*. _____

8. Necesito una *racket* para jugar al tenis. _____

9. Para jugar al fútbol americano necesitamos *helmets*. _____

10. Tengo que comprar un *glove* para jugar al béisbol. _____

5 Choose an appropriate response for each statement.

1. _____ El equipo de Luis gana hoy.
2. _____ A Juan Pablo le gusta nadar.
3. _____ Vamos a la cancha.
4. _____ Patinar en línea es peligroso.
5. _____ Aquí está el bate.
6. _____ Soy atleta.
7. _____ Tengo patines de línea nuevos.
8. _____ Queremos nadar.
9. _____ Tengo que comprar un guante.
10. _____ A Andrea le gusta el tenis.

a. Vamos a la piscina.
b. Voy a patinar en línea.
c. Van a ser los campeones.
d. Vamos a jugar al béisbol.
e. Me gustan los deportes.
f. Vamos a jugar al tenis.
g. La natación es su deporte favorito.
h. Necesito llevar un casco.
i. Va a la cancha para jugar.
j. Voy a la tienda de deportes.

6 Write three sentences telling what your favorite sport is, where you play, and what equipment you need. Follow the model.

Modelo: *Mi deporte favorito es el tenis. Tengo que ir a la cancha para jugar.*
   Necesito una pelota y una raqueta.

_____

_____

_____

Did You Get It? *Presentación de gramática*

 ¡AVANZA!   **Goal:**   Use **jugar** to talk about playing sports.

The Verb jugar

• Study the conjugation of the verb **jugar**.

jugar *(to play)*	
juego	jugamos
juegas	jugáis
juega	juegan

EXPLANATION: Use **jugar** to talk about playing a sport or a game. **Jugar** is a stem-changing verb in which **u** changes to **ue** in all forms except **nosotros(as)** and **vosotros(as)**.

Jugar a + sport

• Read the following sentences, paying attention to the boldfaced words.

Pilar **juega al básquetbol.**   *(Pilar **plays basketball**.)*
Jorge y yo **jugamos al tenis.**   *(Jorge and I **play tennis**.)*
Tú y Ana **jugáis al voleibol.**   *(You and Ana **play volleyball**.)*

EXPLANATION: When you use **jugar** with the name of a sport, use **jugar a + sport**. Remember that **a + el** (masculine article) becomes **al**.

Did You Get It? *Práctica de gramática*

¡AVANZA!	**Goal:** Use **jugar** to talk about playing sports.

1 Write the correct form of **jugar** for each subject.

1. Manuel _____

2. tú _____

3. mi hermano y yo _____

4. ustedes _____

5. yo _____

6. nosotros _____

7. Belén y tú _____

8. los atletas _____

2 Complete each sentence with the correct form of **jugar**.

1. Mis amigos _____ al tenis y al básquetbol.

2. Yo _____ al básquetbol, que es mi deporte favorito.

3. Tu equipo _____ al béisbol en el campo.

4. ¿Te gusta _____ al tenis?

5. Isabel y sus amigas _____ al voleibol.

6. Nosotros no _____ al fútbol americano.

7. ¿ _____ tú en un buen equipo de voleibol?

8. Ustedes _____ al béisbol todos los sábados.

3 Write complete sentences using **jugar**. Follow the model.

Modelo: Juanita / el béisbol / una pelota

   Juanita juega al béisbol con una pelota.

1. nosotros / el tenis / una raqueta

_____

2. los chicos / el voleibol / una pelota

_____

3. los campeones / el béisbol / un bate

_____

4. Tomás y José / el fútbol / una pelota

_____

5. yo / el básquetbol / una pelota

_____

6. tú / el fútbol americano / un casco

_____

4 What are they playing? Write a sentence using **jugar** to describe each picture.

1.   2.   3.   4.

1. _____

2. _____

3. _____

4. _____

5 Translate the following sentences into Spanish.

1. Mario is a good athlete.

_____

2. His team is going to win the game.

_____

3. José and Alfredo are the best players on the team.

_____

4. José has a new bat.

_____

5. Alfredo has a new helmet.

_____

6. All the players wear helmets because the sport is dangerous.

_____

7. All the players on the team play well. They are the champions.

_____

8. The team wins the game, twenty-one to seven.

_____

9. What sport do you play?

_____

Did You Get It? *Presentación de gramática*

| ¡AVANZA! | **Goal:** Learn how to use **saber** and **conocer**, as well as the personal **a**. |

The Verbs saber and conocer

• Read each set of sentences below, paying attention to the boldfaced words.

1. **Sé** cuánto cuesta la raqueta.   (*I know how much the racket costs.*)
   Sabemos que es una buena jugadora.   (*We know that she is a good player.*)

2. **Sabes patinar** muy bien.   (*You know how to skate very well.*)
   ¿**Sabe** Teresa **nadar**?   (*Does Teresa know how to swim?*)

3. **Conozco** la República Dominicana.   (*I know the Dominican Republic.*)
   ¿**Conoces** a mi amigo Daniel?   (*Do you know my friend Daniel?*)

4. ¿Quieres **conocer** a los campeones?   (*Do you want to meet the champions?*)
   Queremos **conocer** a los otros jugadores. (*We want to meet the other players.*)

EXPLANATION: Both **saber** and **conocer** mean *to know*. Use **saber** to (1) talk about factual information. Use **saber** + *infinitive* to (2) say how to do something. Use **conocer** to (3) say that you know or are familiar with a place or a person. Also use **conocer** to (4) talk about meeting someone for the first time.

• Use the chart below as a quick reference for the different forms of **saber** and **conocer**.

saber *(to know)*		conocer *(to know)*	
sé	sabemos	cono*z*co	conocemos
sabes	sabéis	conoces	conocéis
sabe	saben	conoce	conocen

EXPLANATION: **Saber** and **conocer** have irregular **yo** forms.

Did You Get It? *Práctica de gramática*

UNIDAD 6 Lección 1

Reteaching and Practice

| ¡AVANZA! | **Goal:** Learn how to use **saber** and **conocer**, as well as the personal **a**. |

❶ **Saber** or **conocer**? Which would you use to say that you know . . .

1. how to play football? _____
2. Santo Domingo? _____
3. your friend's family? _____
4. how to swim? _____
5. where your cousin lives? _____
6. your neighbor? _____
7. that math is difficult? _____

❷ Create sentences using **conocer** to say who or what these people know.
Follow the model.

Modelo: Ana / Trini Salgado   *Ana conoce a Trini Salgado.*

1. Los aficionados / las campeonas _____
2. yo / los jugadores del equipo _____
3. tú / mi tía _____
4. Amalia y yo / los ganadores del partido _____
5. usted / Santo Domingo _____

❸ Create sentences using **saber** to say what these people know or know how to do.
Follow the model.

Modelo: Felipe / nadar   *Felipe sabe nadar.*

1. Roberto / dónde está la tienda de ropa de deportes

_____

2. yo / cuánto cuesta la raqueta

_____

3. ustedes / patinar en línea

_____

4. tú / jugar al béisbol

_____

5. mis amigos y yo / cuándo empieza el partido

_____

4 Choose the correct verb to complete the email.

Hola, Marisa:

   ¿Cómo estás? ¿(Sabes / Conoces) que mi equipo de voleibol acaba de ganar otro partido? Estamos muy contentas porque (sabemos / conocemos) que vamos a ser las campeonas. En el verano, las otras jugadoras y yo vamos a Santo Domingo. Yo no (conozco / sé) bien la ciudad. Mis amigas tampoco la (conocen / saben). Pero (sé / conozco) que va a ser un viaje interesante. Y tú, ¿(sabes / conoces) qué vas a hacer este verano?

Tu amiga, Eva

5 Complete the sentences with the correct form of **saber** or **conocer**.

1. Tú _____ a Yolanda.

2. Nosotros _____ jugar al fútbol.

3. Ellas _____ que vamos a ganar el partido.

4. Ustedes _____ bien a Juan y a Raúl.

5. Jorge _____ tocar la guitarra y el piano.

6. Yo _____ Santo Domingo; es mi ciudad favorita.

7. Los estudiantes _____ que la escuela es importante.

8. Queremos _____ a los jugadores.

9. Mi madre _____ que quiero un bate nuevo.

10. Miguel no _____ la República Dominicana.

6 Translate the following sentences into Spanish.

1. Julia knows my uncle.

   _____

2. Anita knows how to swim.

   _____

3. I know that my sister is very athletic.

   _____

4. My family knows that I am at the pool.

   _____

5. Andrés knows the players on the team.

   _____

6. They know how to play basketball.

   _____

¿Recuerdas?

Numbers from 200 to 1,000,000

- You have learned how to count from 200 to 1,000,000. Recall how to count by hundreds below.

100	**cien**
200	**doscientos**
300	**trescientos**
400	**cuatrocientos**
500	**quinientos**
600	**seiscientos**
700	**setecientos**
800	**ochocientos**
900	**novecientos**
1,000	**mil**
1,000,000	**un millón (de)**

1 Write out how many **pesos** the following items cost.

2,600 pesos   4,515 pesos   878,400 pesos   2,950 pesos   5,570 pesos   620 pesos

1.   2.   3.   4.   5.   6.

1. _____

2. _____

3. _____

4. _____

5. _____

6. _____

UNIDAD 6 Lección 1
Reteaching and Practice

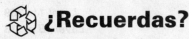 **¿Recuerdas?**

Using *gustar* with nouns

- You use **gustar** to say that you or others like something.

When one thing is liked		When more than one thing is liked	
Me **gusta** el béisbol.	*(I like baseball.)*	Me **gustan** los bates.	*(I like the bats.)*
Te **gusta** el béisbol.	*(You like baseball.)*	Te **gustan** los bates.	*(You like the bats.)*
Le **gusta** el béisbol.	*(He likes baseball.)*	Le **gustan** los bates.	*(He likes the bats.)*
Nos **gusta** el béisbol.	*(We like baseball.)*	Nos **gustan** los bates.	*(We like the bats.)*
Os **gusta** el béisbol.	*(You like baseball.)*	Os **gustan** los bates.	*(You like the bats.)*
Les **gusta** el béisbol.	*(They like baseball.)*	Les **gustan** los bates.	*(They like the bats.)*

EXPLANATION: No matter *who* likes baseball, the verb is always singular (**gusta**), and no matter *who* likes the bats, the verb is always plural (**gustan**). In other words, **gustar** agrees with *what* is liked, not with *who* does the liking.

Práctica

1 Would you use **gusta** or **gustan** in a sentence to say that . . .

1. you like apples? _____
2. they like football? _____
3. she likes the car? _____
4. Juan likes bicyles? _____
5. my parents like tennis? _____

6. everyone likes ice cream? _____
7. my uncle likes sports? _____
8. my aunt likes the theater? _____
9. we like movies? _____
10. I like everything? _____

2 Answer the questions in complete sentences.

1. ¿Te gustan los deportes? _____
2. ¿Te gusta el básquetbol? _____
3. ¿Te gusta el voleibol? _____
4. ¿Te gustan los partidos de tenis? _____
5. ¿Te gustan las piscinas? _____

3 Translate the following sentences.

1. I like this racket. _____
2. The team likes the swimming pool. _____
3. We like this baseball field. _____
4. They like all sports. _____

UNIDAD 6 Lección 1   Reteaching and Practice

UNIDAD 6 Lección 1

Reteaching and Practice

♻ ¿Recuerdas?

Comparatives

• You have learned how to make comparisons in Spanish. Review the phrases below.

Phrases with an *adjective* to compare two things:

más... que	*(more . . . than)*
menos... que	*(less . . . than)*
tan... como	*(as . . . as)*

Phrases to compare two actions:

más que...	*(more than . . .)*
menos que...	*(less than . . .)*
tanto como...	*(as much as . . .)*

Irregular comparative words:

mayor	*(older)*	**menor**	*(younger)*
mejor	*(better)*	**peor**	*(worse)*

Práctica

1 Write sentences telling which sport you think is more difficult. Follow the model.

Modelo: swimming / tennis *La natación es más difícil que el tenis.*

1. football / tennis _____

2. baseball / basketball _____

3. basketball / tennis _____

4. volleyball / swimming _____

5. baseball / soccer _____

2 Write sentences telling which sport you prefer. Follow the model.

Modelo: baseball / volleyball *Me gusta el béisbol menos que el voleibol.*

1. tennis / baseball _____

2. football / basketball _____

3. volleyball / tennis _____

4. basketball / baseball _____

5. baseball / volleyball _____

Nombre ______________________ Clase ______________ Fecha ______________

Did You Get It? *Presentación de vocabulario*

Level 1 pp. 326–327
Level 1B p. 132–134

¡AVANZA! **Goal:** Learn how to talk about staying healthy and about parts of the body.

Staying Healthy

- Good health (**la buena salud**) is important for everyone. There are many things you can do to stay healthy (**sano**) and to avoid being hurt (**herido**) or sick (**enfermo**).

  If you live near the sea **(el mar)** you can scuba dive **(bucear)** and water ski **(hacer esquí acuático).** You can also jog or walk (**caminar**) on the beach (**la playa**). To stay strong (**fuerte**), you can to lift weights (**levantar pesas**). If your body begins to to hurt (**doler**), it's time to take a break and to sunbathe (**tomar el sol**). Don't forget the sun screen (**el bloqueador de sol**)!

Parts Of The Body

- Read the names for the different parts of the body.

(THE HEAD) **LA CABEZA**

(THE BODY) **EL CUERPO**

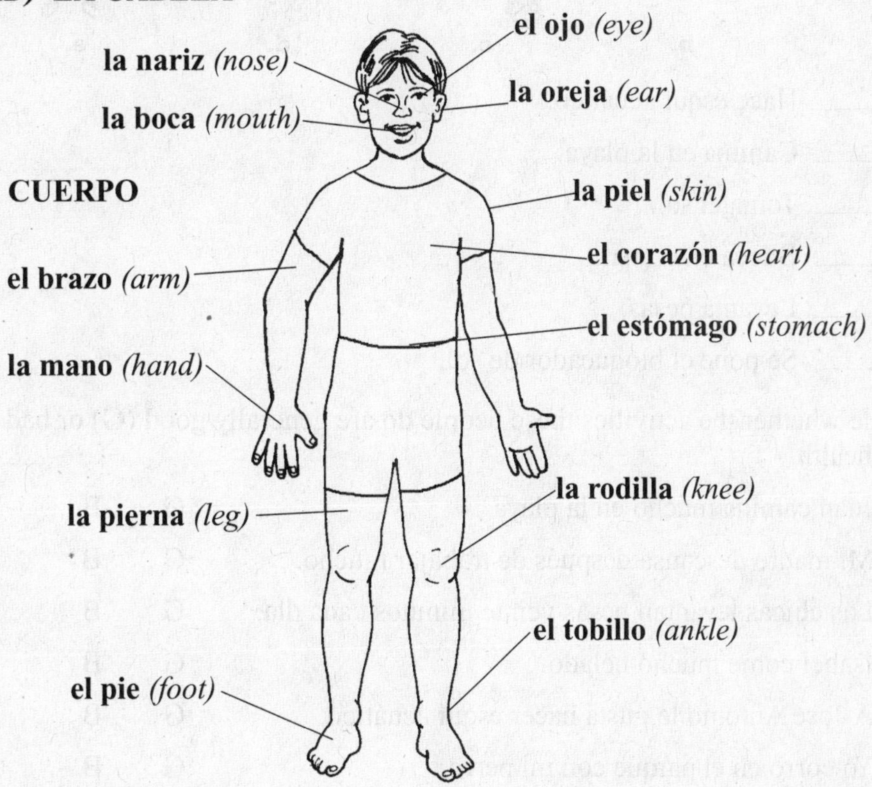
el ojo (eye)
la nariz (nose)
la oreja (ear)
la boca (mouth)
la piel (skin)
el corazón (heart)
el brazo (arm)
el estómago (stomach)
la mano (hand)
la rodilla (knee)
la pierna (leg)
el tobillo (ankle)
el pie (foot)

Did You Get It? *Práctica de vocabulario*

¡AVANZA!   **Goal:** Learn how to talk about staying healthy and about parts of the body.

1 Which body part do you use to . . .

1. kick a soccer ball? _____
2. talk to your friends? _____
3. digest your lunch? _____
4. watch television? _____
5. hug your friend? _____

6. write an e–mail? _____
7. think? _____
8. kneel? _____
9. smell? _____

2 Choose the sentence that describes what each person is doing.

a.   b.   c.   d.   e.   f.

1. _____ Hace esquí acuático.
2. _____ Camina en la playa.
3. _____ Toma el sol.
4. _____ Bucea en el mar.
5. _____ Levanta pesas.
6. _____ Se pone el bloqueador de sol.

3 Decide whether the activities these people do are generally good (**G**) or bad (**B**) for their health.

1. Juan camina mucho en la playa.   G   B
2. Mi madre descansa después de trabajar mucho.   G   B
3. Las chicas levantan pesas veinte minutos cada día. G   B
4. Isabel come mucho helado.   G   B
5. A José Antonio le gusta hacer esquí acuático.   G   B
6. Yo corro en el parque con mi perro.   G   B
7. Nunca usamos el bloqueador de sol.   G   B
8. Álex prefiere dormir tres horas cada noche.   G   B

3 Choose appropriate vocabulary words to complete this conversation between two friends.

Melinda: Tú sabes que la buena _____ es importante para nosotras y para todos. Nadie quiere estar enfermo o _____ .

Juana: ¿Qué podemos hacer para estar _____ ?

Melinda: Podemos hacer muchas actividades. Como vivimos cerca del _____ , podemos _____ , bucear o hacer esquí _____ .

Juana: Tienes razón. Y también podemos caminar en la _____.

Melinda: Y si queremos ser _____ , podemos...

Juana: ...¡levantar _____ !

4 Translate the following sentences into Spanish.

1. We walk to be healthy.

_____

2. We put on sunscreen when we sunbathe.

_____

3. Anita waterskis in the sea.

_____

4. My stomach hurts.

_____

5. Jorge and David are strong because they lift weights.

_____

5 Imagine that you live near the sea. Write three activities that you can do every day to stay strong and healthy.

_____

_____

Did You Get It? *Presentación de gramática*

Level 1 p. 331
Level 1B p. 138

¡AVANZA!	**Goal:** Learn to use the preterite tense of regular **-ar** verbs

The Preterite Tense

• Read the conversations below, paying close attention to the boldfaced words.

—¿Siempre **bailas** mucho?   (*Do you always dance a lot?*)

—No, pero anoche **bailé** toda la noche.   (*No, but I danced all last night.*)

—¿Ustedes siempre **nadan** en el mar?   (*Do you always swim in the sea?*)

—No, ayer **nadamos** en la piscina.   (*No, we swam in the pool yesterday.*)

EXPLANATION: The **preterite** is used to express an action completed at a definite time in the past. It is usually referred to as the *past tense* in English. In English, regular verbs in the past tense, such as *danced,* end in *–ed.* Others, such as *swam,* are irregular.

Conjugating -ar Verbs in the Preterite

• Study the conjugation of **caminar** to learn the preterite endings for all regular **-ar** verbs.

caminar (to walk)	
caminé	caminamos
caminaste	caminasteis
caminó	caminaron

EXPLANATION: The preterite tense of regular **-ar** verbs is formed by adding these endings to the stem: **-é, -aste, -ó, -amos, -asteis, -aron**. Notice that the **yo** and **él/ella/usted** forms have an accent over the final vowel.

• Study these sentences.

Caminamos en la playa.   **Caminamos** en la playa ayer.
(We walk on the beach.)   *(We walked on the beach yesterday.)*

EXPLANATION: The **nosotros(as)** form is the same in the preterite and the present tenses. Context clues, such as **ayer** (*yesterday*), help you to know whether the verb is in the preterite and the present tenses.

Did You Get It? *Práctica de gramática*

¡AVANZA!   **Goal:**   Learn to use the preterite tense of regular **-ar** verbs

① Write the correct preterite form for each verb.

1. yo (nadar) _____
2. ustedes (tomar) _____
3. nosotros (cantar) _____
4. él (hablar) _____
5. Tomás (bucear) _____

6. las chicas (estudiar) _____
7. vosotros (trabajar) _____
8. tú (caminar) _____
9. Alex y yo (nadar) _____
10. usted (levantar) _____

② Complete each sentence with the correct preterite form of the verb in parentheses.

1. Mi equipo favorito _____ el partido. (ganar)
2. Tú _____ al centro comercial. (caminar)
3. José _____ el almuerzo. (preparar)
4. María y yo _____ los platos. (lavar)
5. ¿_____ ustedes los discos compactos? (encontrar)
6. Ustedes _____ en el mar. (bucear)
7. Yo _____ mucho ayer. (trabajar)
8. Mis amigos y yo _____ mucho en la fiesta. (bailar)
9. Ellos _____ por teléfono ayer. (hablar)
10. ¿_____ ustedes el sol en la playa? (tomar)

③ Rewrite each sentence in the preterite tense. Follow the model.

Modelo: Ellas caminan en la playa hoy.   *Ellas caminaron en la playa ayer.*

1. Miguel nada en el mar hoy. _____
2. Mi hermana y yo tomamos el sol hoy. _____
3. Ustedes levantan pesas hoy. _____
4. Yo monto en bicicleta hoy. _____
5. Tú compras zapatos nuevos hoy. _____
6. Ana y yo buceamos en el mar hoy. _____
7. Usted mira la televisión hoy. _____
8. Decoramos la sala para la fiesta hoy. _____
9. La chica usa la computadora hoy. _____
10. Ayudo a mi madre con la cena hoy. _____

UNIDAD 6 Lección 2   **Reteaching and Practice**

4 Use the verbs in the box to complete the e–mail in the preterite tense.

| tomar | pasar | caminar | bucear | descansar |

Hola, Emiliana:

Ayer mis amigos y yo **1.** _____ el día en la playa. Yo
2. _____ los sándwiches y Jorge y Linda **3.** _____
los refrescos. Ellos **4.** _____ en el mar. A mí no me gusta bucear.
Yo **5.** _____ el sol y **6.** _____ . Después de comer,
nosotros **7.** _____ . Y tú, Emiliana, **8.** ¿ _____ en
la playa ayer?

Tu amiga,
Lisa

5 Translate the following sentences into Spanish.

   1. Felicia listened to music. _____

   2. The team won the game. _____

   3. We sunbathed yesterday. _____

   4. Jorge and María rested at home. _____

   5. I lifted weights. _____

   6. The athletes skated in the park. _____

   7. You watched television. _____

   8. The champions played baseball. _____

   9. David talked on the telephone with Isa. _____

   10. You (*ustedes*) walked to school. _____

6 Write five sentences using any regular **-ar** verbs to tell what you and the following people did yesterday.

   1. yo _____

   2. mi mejor amigo(a) _____

   3. mis padres _____

   4. mis amigos y yo _____

   5. mi maestro(a) de español _____

Did You Get It? *Presentación de gramática*

> **¡AVANZA!**   **Goal:** Learn the preterite forms for verbs ending in **-car**, **-gar**, and **-zar**.

Preterite Forms of *-car*, *-gar*, and *-zar* Verbs

- Read the following sentences, paying close attention to the boldfaced words.

Yo **toqué** la guitarra ayer.
(I played the guitar yesterday.)

Ellos **tocaron** la guitarra ayer.
(They played the guitar yesterday.)

Yo **jugué** al béisbol.
(I played baseball.)

Ella **jugó** al béisbol.
(She played baseball.)

Yo **almorcé** en casa.
(I ate at home.)

Vosotros **almorzasteis** en casa.
(You all ate at home.)

EXPLANATION: Regular verbs that end in **-car**, **-gar**, and **-zar** have a spelling change in the **yo** form of the preterite. The change allows the words to maintain their original sound. Study the conjugation of **tocar**, **pagar,** and **comenzar**. Use the chart as a quick reference for the preterite tense of these verbs.

	tocar *(to play)*	pagar *(to pay)*	comenzar *(to begin)*
yo	**toqué**	**pagué**	**comencé**
tú	**tocaste**	**pagaste**	**comenzaste**
él/ella/usted	**tocó**	**pagó**	**comenzó**
nosotros(as)	**tocamos**	**pagamos**	**comenzamos**
vosotros(as)	**tocasteis**	**pagasteis**	**comenzasteis**
ellos(as)/ ustedes	**tocaron**	**pagaron**	**comenzaron**

Did You Get It? *Práctica de gramática*

> **¡AVANZA!** **Goal:** Learn the preterite forms for verbs ending in **-car**, **-gar**, and **-zar**.

1 Write the preterite **yo** form of each verb.

1. buscar _____
2. almorzar _____
3. tocar _____
4. practicar _____
5. jugar _____
6. comenzar _____
7. sacar _____
8. llegar _____

2 Complete the paragraph with the correct preterite form of the verb in parentheses to know what Juan did this morning.

Esta mañana **1.** _____ (levantarme) a las seis y media. **2.** _____ (levantar) pesas por media hora. Mi madre me **3.** _____ (preparar) un buen desayuno. Después de desayunar, **4.** _____ (buscar) mis libros y **5.** _____ (caminar) a la escuela con mi hermano. Nosotros **6.** _____ (caminar) rápido porque no nos gusta llegar tarde. Mi primera clase **7.** _____ (empezar) a las ocho, y mi última clase **8.** _____ (terminar) a las dos y media. Después, **9.** _____ (jugar) un rato al fútbol con mis amigos. **10.** _____ (llegar) a casa a las cinco y media. A las seis y media **11.** _____ (cenar), y antes de dormir **12.** _____ (tocar) un rato la guitarra.

3 Use the correct preterite form of the verbs in the box to complete the following sentences.

practicar	llegar	tocar	empezar	almorzar
sacar	nadar	jugar	caminar	buscar

1. Después de las clases, yo _____ el piano.
2. Roberto y yo _____ en el nuevo restaurante.
3. ¿_____ ustedes en la piscina de la escuela?
4. ¿A qué hora _____ béisbol los chicos ?
5. Yo _____ al tenis con mi hermana.
6. ¿Por qué _____ ellos a la playa?
7. La película _____ a las siete y media.
8. Mis abuelos _____ una nueva casa.
9. Antonio _____ buenas notas el semestre pasado.
10. ¿_____ yo demasiado temprano?

4 Answer the following questions in complete sentences to explain what you did today.

1. ¿Llegaste temprano a la escuela?

   _____

2. ¿Almorzaste en la cafetería?

   _____

3. ¿Practicaste deportes?

   _____

4. ¿Tocaste un instrumento musical?

   _____

5. ¿Buscaste a tus amigos?

   _____

5 Translate the following sentences into Spanish.

1. I played volleyball yesterday.

   _____

2. I ate a good lunch.

   _____

3. We danced at the party.

   _____

4. I played the guitar for my father.

   _____

5. Julio, did you study for the history test?

   _____

6. José spoke with Juanita about the problem.

   _____

7. The boys played soccer on the field.

   _____

8. I got a bad grade in mathematics.

   _____

9. My sister and I prepared dinner last night.

   _____

10. Did you all sunbathe at the beach?

   _____

♻ ¿Recuerdas?

Level 1 p. 330
Level 1B p. 137

Using Gustar with Nouns

• You already know that to say what you or someone likes you use **gustar** + a noun. To review, read the following sentences, paying attention to the boldfaced words.

  Me **gusta** la playa. *(I like the beach.)*

  Me **gustan** las bicicletas. *(I like bicycles.)*

EXPLANATION: Remember that the verb **gustar** agrees in number with *what* is liked and not with *who* is doing the liking.

_____

Práctica

❶ Complete each sentence with the correct form of **gustar**. Then translate the sentences into English.

1. ¿A Alicia le _____ el fútbol? _____

2. Me _____ todos los deportes. _____

3. ¿Te _____ el mar? _____

4. A Susana y a mí nos _____ la música. _____

5. A Pedro le _____ la playa. _____

6. A las chicas les _____ los patines. _____

7. Me _____ este bloqueador de sol. _____

8. ¿A ustedes les _____ el sol? _____

9. A Linda le _____ la bicicleta roja. _____

10. No les _____ las raquetas nuevas. _____

❷ Translate the following sentences into Spanish.

1. We like all beaches. _____

2. My sister and I like baseball. _____

3. He likes this sunscreen. _____

4. Do you (**ustedes**) like sports? _____

5. My cousin likes water sports. _____

6. I like the sea. _____

7. We like volleyball. _____

8. Does Alicia like the new bats? _____

9. They don't like the sun. _____

10. My friends like basketball. _____

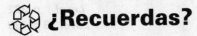

Level 1 p. 330
Level 1B p. 137

♻ ¿Recuerdas?

Stem Changing Verbs: o —→ ue

• Study the conjugation of **volver** (*to come back*).

volver *(to return)*	
vuelvo	volvemos
vuelves	volvéis
vuelve	vuelven

EXPLANATION: Volver is an **o —→ ue** stem-changing verb. The stem changes from **o** to **ue** in all forms except **nosotros(as)** and **vosotros(as)**. Other verbs that follow the same pattern are **doler** (*to hurt*), **poder** (*to be able*), **almorzar** (*to eat lunch*), **encontrar** (*to find*), and **dormir** (*to sleep*).

Práctica

❶ Complete the sentences with the correct form of the verb in parentheses.

1. Tú _____ nadar. (poder)

2. ¿Te _____ las piernas? (doler)

3. Carla y Eduardo _____ en el restaurante. (almorzar)

4. Juan _____ a casa a las seis para comer. (volver)

5. Mi hermana y yo _____ en el autobús. (dormir)

6. Me _____ la cabeza. (doler)

7. ¿_____ ustedes el teatro? (encontrar)

8. Ustedes _____ a casa mañana. (volver)

❷ Write sentences using the following words. Follow the model.

Modelo: tú / dormir / en casa de tu amigo   *Tú duermes en casa de tu amigo.*

1. a mí / doler / la cabeza _____

2. tú / encontrar / los libros _____

3. nosotros / volver / para almorzar _____

4. él / poder / bailar bien _____

5. yo / almorzar / a las once y media _____

6. a Elena / doler / el estómago _____

7. los chicos / poder / cocinar esta noche _____

8. usted / almorzar / a la una y media _____

UNIDAD 6 Lección 2
Reteaching and Practice

¿Recuerdas?

Level 1 p. 332
Level 1B p. 139

Telling Time

- Review ways to talk about time in Spanish. Study the following.

Son las nueve.	*(It's 9 o'clock.)*
Desayuné a las ocho menos diez.	*(I ate breakfast at 7:50.)*
Es la una y veinte.	*(It's 1:20.)*
Almorcé a la una.	*(I ate lunch at 1 o'clock.)*
Son las siete y media.	*(It's 7:30.)*
Cené a las seis y cuarto.	*(I ate dinner at 6:15.)*

Práctica

1 Write the time in Spanish. The first one is done for you.

    1. 11:30   *Son las once y media.*

    2. 6:15 _____

    3. 8:05 _____

    4. 4:55 _____

    5. 3:30 _____

    6. 12:00 _____

    7. 9:12 _____

    8. 2:45 _____

    9. 10:00 _____

    10. 7:15 _____

2 Answer the questions in complete sentences to say at what time you did certain activities today.

    1. ¿A qué hora desayunaste? _____

    2. ¿A qué hora llegaste a la escuela? _____

    3. ¿A qué hora fuiste a la clase de español? _____

    4. ¿A qué hora almorzaste? _____

    5. ¿A qué hora cenaste? _____

Did You Get It? Answer Key

Did You Get It? Answer

PRÁCTICA DE VOCABULARIO
SPORTS, pp. 2–3

1
1. el bate
2. la raqueta
3. el casco
4. la pelota
5. los patines en línea

2
1. la cancha
2. el campo
3. la piscina
4. la cancha
5. la cancha
6. el estadio

3
1. el básquetbol, la pelota
2. el tenis, la raqueta
3. el béisbol, el bate, la pelota, el casco
4. el voleibol, la pelota
5. patinaje en línea, los patines en línea

4
1. las reglas   2. aficionados
3. ganar   4. perder
5. atleta   6. jugadora
7. peligroso   8. raqueta
9. cascos   10. guante

5
1. c   2. g
3. f   4. h
5. d   6. e
7. b   8. a
9. j   10. i

6 Answers will vary.

PRÁCTICA DE GRAMÁTICA
THE VERB **JUGAR**, pp. 5–6

1
1. juega
2. juegas
3. jugamos
4. juegan
5. juego
6. jugamos
7. juegan
8. juegan

2
1. juegan
2. juego
3. juega
4. jugar
5. juegan
6. jugamos
7. Juegas
8. juegan

3
1. Nosotros jugamos al tenis con una raqueta.
2. Los chicos juegan al voleibol con una pelota.
3. Los campeones juegan al béisbol con un bate.
4. Tomás y José juegan al fútbol con una pelota.
5. Yo juego al básquetbol con una pelota.
6. Tú juegas al fútbol americano con un casco.

UNIDAD 6 Lección 1
Reteaching and Practice Answer Key

Did You Get It? Answer Key

4

1. Las chicas juegan al voleibol.
2. El equipo juega al béisbol. / Juegan al béisbol.
3. Los chicos juegan al tenis.
4. La chica juega al fútbol.

5

1. Mario es un buen atleta.
2. Su equipo va a ganar el partido.
3. José y Alfredo son los mejores jugadores del equipo.
4. José tiene un bate nuevo.
5. Alfredo tiene un casco nuevo.
6. Todos los jugadores llevan cascos porque el deporte es peligroso.
7. Todos los jugadores del equipo juegan bien. Son los campeones.
8. El equipo gana el partido, veintiuno a siete.
9. ¿A qué deporte juegas tú?

PRÁCTICA DE GRAMÁTICA

THE VERBS **SABER** AND **CONOCER**, pp. 8–9

1

1. saber
2. conocer
3. conocer
4. saber
5. saber
6. conocer
7. saber

2

1. Los aficionados conocen a las campeonas.
2. Yo conozco a los jugadores del equipo.
3. Tú conoces a mi tía.
4. Amalia y yo conocemos a los ganadores del partido.
5. Usted conoce Santo Domingo.

3

1. Roberto sabe dónde está la tienda de ropa de deportes.
2. Yo sé cuánto cuesta la raqueta.
3. Ustedes saben patinar en línea.
4. Tú sabes jugar al béisbol.
5. Mis amigos y yo sabemos cuándo empieza el partido.

4

Hola, Marisa:

¿Cómo estás? ¿**Sabes** que mi equipo de voleibol acaba de ganar otro partido? Estamos muy contentas porque **sabemos** que vamos a ser las campeonas. En el verano, las otras jugadoras y yo vamos a Santo Domingo. Yo no **conozco** bien la ciudad. Mis amigas tampoco la **conocen**. Pero **sé** que va a ser un viaje interesante. Y tú, ¿**sabes** qué vas a hacer este verano?

  Tu amiga, Eva

5

1. conoces
2. sabemos
3. saben
4. conocen
5. sabe
6. conozco
7. saben
8. conocer
9. sabe
10. conoce

6

1. Julia conoce a mi tío.
2. Anita sabe nadar.
3. Sé que mi hermana es muy atlética.
4. Mi familia sabe que estoy en la piscina.
5. Andrés conoce a los jugadores del equipo.
6. Ellos saben jugar al básquetbol.

Did You Get It? Answer Key

✿ ¿RECUERDAS?

NUMBERS FROM 200 TO 1,000,000, p. 10

1

1. dos mil seiscientos pesos
2. cuatro mil quinientos setenta y cinco pesos
3. ochocientos setenta y ocho mil, cuatrocientos pesos
4. dos mil novecientos cincuenta pesos
5. cinco mil quinientos setenta pesos
6. seiscientos veinte pesos

✿ ¿RECUERDAS?

USING **GUSTAR** WITH NOUNS, p. 10

1

1. gustan	2. gusta
3. gusta	4. gustan
5. gusta	6. gusta
7. gustan	8. gusta
9. gustan	10. gusta

2

1. Sí, (No, no) me gustan los deportes.
2. Sí, (No, no) me gusta el básquetbol.
3. Sí, (No, no) me gusta el voleibol.
4. Sí, (No, no) me gustan los partidos de tenis.
5. Sí, (No, no) me gustan las piscinas.

3

1. Me gusta esta raqueta.
2. Al equipo le gusta la piscina.
3. Nos gusta este campo de béisbol.
4. A ellos les gustan todos los deportes.

✿ ¿RECUERDAS?

COMPARATIVES, p. 12

1 Answers will vary.

2 Answers will vary.

Did You Get It? Answer Key

PRÁCTICA DE VOCABULARIO
STAYING HEALTHY AND PARTS OF THE BODY, pp. 14–15

❶

1. el pie
2. la boca
3. el estómago
4. los ojos
5. los brazos
6. las manos
7. la cabeza
8. las rodillas
9. la nariz

❷

1. b
2. c
3. f
4. a
5. e
6. d

❸

1. G
2. G
3. G
4. B
5. G
6. G
7. B
8. B

❸

Melinda: Tú sabes que la buena **salud** es importante para nosotras y para todos. Nadie quiere estar enfermo o **herido**.

Juana: ¿Qué podemos hacer para estar **sanas**?

Melinda: Podemos hacer muchas actividades. Como vivimos cerca del **mar**, podemos **nadar**, bucear o hacer esquí **acuático**.

Juana: Tienes razón. Y también podemos caminar en la **playa**.

Melinda: Y si queremos ser **fuertes**, podemos...

Juana: ...¡levantar **pesas**!

❹

1. Caminamos para estar sanos.
2. Nos ponemos el bloqueador de sol cuando tomamos el sol.
3. Anita hace esquí acuático en el mar.
4. Me duele el estómago.
5. Jorge y Davíd son fuertes porque levantan pesas.

❺ Answers will vary.

PRÁCTICA DE VOCABULARIO
THE PRETERITE TENSE OF REGULAR –AR VERBS, pp. 17–18

❶

1. nadé
2. tomaron
3. cantamos
4. habló
5. buceó
6. estudiaron
7. trabajasteis
8. caminaste
9. nadamos
10. levantó

❷

1. ganó
2. caminaste
3. preparó
4. lavamos
5. Encontraron
6. bucearon
7. trabajé
8. bailamos
9. hablaron
10. Tomaron

❸

1. Miguel nadó en el mar ayer.
2. Mi hermana y yo tomamos el sol ayer.
3. Ustedes levantaron pesas ayer.
4. Yo monté en bicicleta ayer.
5. Tú compraste zapatos nuevos ayer.
6. Ana y yo buceamos en el mar ayer.
7. Usted miró la televisión ayer.
8. Decoramos la sala para la fiesta ayer.
9. La chica usó la computadora ayer.
10. Ayudé a mi madre con la cena ayer.

Did You Get It? Answer Key

4

Hola, Emiliana:

Ayer mis amigos y yo **pasamos** el día en la playa. Yo **llevé** los sándwiches y Jorge y Linda **llevaron** los refrescos. Ellos **bucearon** en el mar. A mí no me gusta bucear. Yo **tomé** el sol y **descansé**. Después de comer, nosotros **caminamos**. Y tú, Emiliana, ¿**caminaste** en la playa ayer?

Tu amiga,
Lisa

5

1. Felicia escuchó música.
2. El equipo ganó el partido.
3. Nosotros tomamos el sol ayer.
4. Jorge y María descansaron en su casa.
5. Yo levanté pesas.
6. Los atletas patinaron en el parque.
7. Tú miraste la televisión.
8. Los campeones jugaron al béisbol.
9. David habló por teléfono con Isa.
10. Ustedes caminaron a la escuela.

6 Answers will vary.

PRÁCTICA DE GRAMÁTICA
THE PRETERITE OF VERBS ENDING IN **–CAR**, **–GAR**, AND **–ZAR**, pp. 20–21

1

1. busqué
2. almorcé
3. toqué
4. practiqué
5. jugué
6. comencé
7. saqué
8. llegué

2

Esta mañana **me levanté** a las seis y media. **Levanté** pesas por media hora. Mi madre me **preparó** un buen desayuno. Después de desayunar, **busqué** mis libros y **caminé** a la escuela con mi hermano. Nosotros **caminamos** rápido porque no nos gusta llegar tarde. Mi primera clase **empezó** a las ocho, y mi última clase **terminó** a las dos y media. Después, **jugué** un rato al fútbol con mis amigos. **Llegué** a casa a las cinco y media. A las seis y media **cené**, y antes de dormir **toqué** un rato la guitarra.

3

1. toqué
2. almorzamos
3. Nadaron
4. practicaron
5. jugué
6. caminaron
7. empezó
8. buscaron
9. sacó
10. Llegué

4 Answers will vary.

5

1. Jugué al voleibol ayer.
2. Almorcé bien.
3. Bailamos en la fiesta.
4. Toqué la guitarra para mi papá.
5. Julio, ¿estudiaste para el examen de historia?
6. José habló con Juanita sobre el problema.
7. Los chicos jugaron al fútbol en el campo.
8. Saqué una mala nota en las matemáticas.
9. Mi hermana y yo preparamos la cena anoche.
10. ¿Tomaron ustedes el sol en la playa?

Did You Get It? Answer Key

 ¿RECUERDAS?

USING **GUSTAR** WITH NOUNS, p. 22

Práctica

1. gusta; Does Alice like football?
2. gustan; I like all sports.
3. gusta; Do you like the sea?
4. gusta; Susana and I like music.
5. gusta; Pedro likes the beach.
6. gustan; The girls like the skates.
7. gusta; I like this sunscreen.
8. gusta; Do you like the sun?
9. gusta; Linda likes the red bicycle.
10. gustan; They don't like the new rackets.

2

1. Nos gustan todas las playas.
2. A mi hermana y a mí nos gusta el béisbol.
3. Le gustan este bloqueador de sol.
4. ¿Les gustan los deportes?
5. A mi primo le gustan los deportes acuáticos.
6. Me gusta el mar.
7. Nos gusta el voleibol.
8. ¿A Alicia le gustan los bates nuevos?
9. A ellos no les gusta el sol.
10. A mis amigos les gusta el básquetbol.

¿RECUERDAS?

STEM–CHANGING VERBS: **O → UE**, p. 23

Práctica

1

1. puedes   2. duelen
3. almuerzan   4. vuelve
5. dormimos   6. duele
7. Encuentran   8. vuelven

 2

1. A mí me duele la cabeza.
2. Tú encuentras los libros.
3. Nosotros volvemos para almorzar.
4. Él puede bailar bien.
5. Yo almuerzo a las once y media.
6. A Elena le duele el estómago.
7. Los chicos pueden cocinar esta noche.
8. Usted almuerza a la una y media.

¿RECUERDAS?

TELLING TIME, p. 24

Práctica

1

1. *Son las once y media.*
2. Son las seis y cuarto.
3. Son las ocho y cinco.
4. Son las cinco menos cinco.
5. Son las tres y media.
6. Son las doce.
7. Son las nueve y doce.
8. Son las tres menos cuarto.
9. Son las diez.
10. Son las siete y cuarto.

2 Answers will vary.

¡Más largo! *Práctica de vocabulario*

Find two words from the **Vocabulario** that contain the same letters as the sequence and belong to the category stated.

	Sequence	Category	Answer
1.	NAR	verbs	_____
2.	ETA	sports people	_____
3.	DOR	adjectives	_____
4.	DER	verbs	_____
5.	CAM	sports words	_____
6.	BOL	sports	_____

¡Cuadrangular! *Vocabulario en contexto*

It's your turn at bat. You hit a home run! In order to round the bases, you must answer each clue around the base path. Each clue contains a boxed letter. Put the letters together to form a secret word. (Hint: Letters are not in order and may be used more than once.)

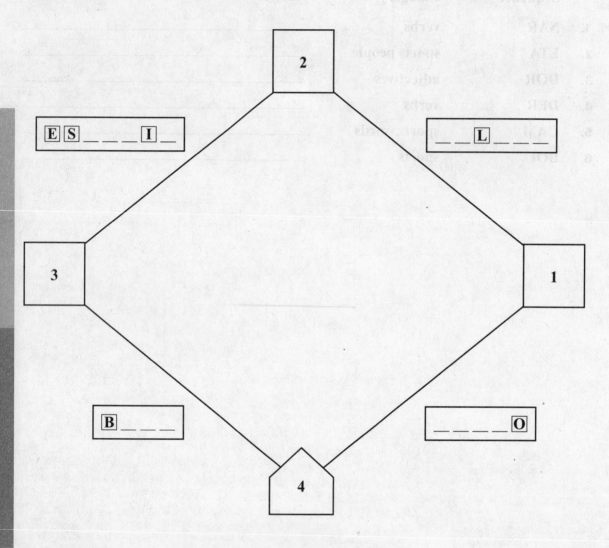

CLUES:

1. El terreno donde se juega un deporte como el fútbol. El...

2. Otra palabra que significa (*means*) bola. La...

3. El lugar donde se sientan (*sit*) los espectadores (*spectators*). El...

4. Le pegas a la bola con esta cosa. El...

Secret word: ____ ____ ____ ____ ____ ____ ____ ____

Practice Games

UNIDAD 6 Lección 1

Copyright © by McDougal Littell, a division of Houghton Mifflin Company.

Comer y jugar *Práctica de gramática 1*

On the left are food items that appear on a menu. On the right are forms of the verb **jugar** with missing letters. Write the forms of the verb **jugar** in the blanks. Some letters are provided. Then use the code numbers below the letters to find a message about what you shouldn't do with your food!

1. J u g o
2

yo ___ ___ e ___ ___
4

2. T o r t a s   d e   j a m ó n
12

tú ___ ___ ___ g ___ ___
3

3. T a c o s   d e   g u a j o l o t e (pavo)
8   5

él/ella/usted ___ ___ ___ ___ a
6

4. H a m b u r g u e s a s
7

nosotros j ___ ___ ___ ___ ___
10

5. E s p a g u e t i s
13   9

vosotros j ___ ___ ___ ___ ___
11

6. G e l a t i n a
11

ellos(as)/ustedes j u ___ ___ ___ ___
1

___ ___ ___ ___ ___ ___ ___ ___ ___ ___ ___
1   2   3   4   5   6   4   5   7   8   2   1

___ ___ ___ ___ ___ ___ ___ ___
9   4   8   2   10 11 12 13

UNIDAD 6 Lección 1   Practice Games

Crucigrama *Gramática en contexto*

Use the correct form of the verb **jugar** to complete the sentences and fill in the crossword puzzle.

Horizontal (*across*)

1. Nosotros _____ al básquetbol en el gimnasio.

3. Yo _____ todos los deportes.

5. Tú _____ fútbol americano en el estadio.

Abajo (*down*)

1. Natalia y Olivia _____ al tenis en el club.

2. Arnaldo _____ al béisbol con un equipo rojo.

4. Vosotros _____ al voleibol con mi hermana Alicia.

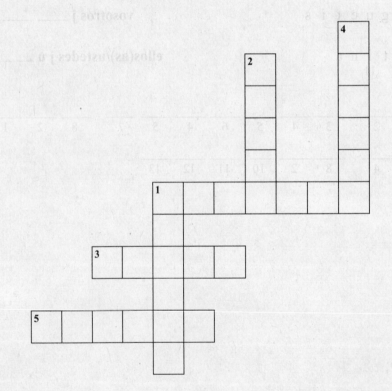

Tic-Tac-Toe *Práctica de gramática 2*

Alone or taking turns with a friend, find the forms of **saber** and **conocer** in the boxes to see who wins at Tic-Tac-Toe. Place an **X** on the board over the correct answer for number 1. Then allow a partner to place an **O** over number 2. Play until someone has won.

X	**O**
1. Yo _____ a la prima de Celia.	2. Tú _____ jugar al tenis.
3. Nosotros _____ cocinar.	4. Las estudiantes _____ Nueva York.
5. Yo _____ la respuesta (*answer*).	6. Mi tía _____ a tu abuela.
7. Tú _____ a la maestra.	8. Vosotros _____ nadar bien.

sabemos	conocen	conozco
conoces	conoce	conocéis
sabes	sabéis	sé

Who won? _____

UNIDAD 6 Lección 1   Practice Games

Algo en común *Todo junto*

Read the clues to figure out what all of the sports have in common. The answers are words related to sports. If you answer correctly, the letters in the boxes form the answer to the final clue. Good luck!

1. Se juega al tenis en este lugar: Es la...
2. Un deporte que se juega con los pies (*feet*) es el...
3. Dos personas o más pueden jugar este deporte. Es el...
4. A veces contiene el apellido o el número del jugador. Es la...
5. Los jugadores forman un grupo o un...
6. El béisbol se juega en un...
7. Este deporte se practica en una piscina. Es la...
8. Se ponen en los pies. Son los...
9. La persona que practica un deporte es la...
10. Se juega este deporte con un balón. Es el...
11. Solamente dos o cuatro personas pueden practicar este deporte. Es el...

FINAL CLUE:

Todos los deportes tienen estos ____ ____ ____ ____ ____ ____ ____ ____ ____ ____ ____

1. ☐ ____ ____ ____ ____

2. ☐ ____ ____ ____ ____

3. ____ ____ ____ ☐ ____ ____ ____

4. ☐ ____ ____ ____ ____ ____ ____

5. ____ ____ ____ ☐ ____ ____ ____

6. ____ ____ ☐ ____ ____

7. ____ ____ ☐ ____ ____ ____ ____

8. ____ ____ ☐ ____ ____

9. ____ ____ ☐ ____ ____ ____

10. ____ ____ ____ ☐ ____ ____ ____ ____

11. ____ ____ ☐ ____ ____ ____

Deportes favoritos *Lectura*

Read the clues to guess each person's favorite sport and write it on the line. Then, draw a picture to represent the sport in the box provided.

1. A Anita no le gusta llevar un casco. No juega un deporte peligroso. No practica con un equipo. A ella le gusta estar en el agua. El deporte favorito de Anita es

_____ .

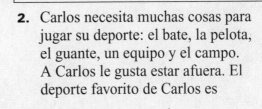

2. Carlos necesita muchas cosas para jugar su deporte: el bate, la pelota, el guante, un equipo y el campo. A Carlos le gusta estar afuera. El deporte favorito de Carlos es

_____ .

3. En su deporte favorito, Laura corre mucho en una cancha. El equipo tiene solamente una jugadora. Usa una raqueta para ganar los partidos. El deporte favorito de Laura es

_____ .

4. Mario y Cristian juegan su deporte favorito en una cancha al aire libre con sus amigos y dentro de un gimnasio con el equipo escolar. Mario quiere ser más alto porque piensa que puede jugar mejor. El deporte favorito de Mario y Cristian es

_____ .

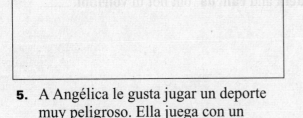

5. A Angélica le gusta jugar un deporte muy peligroso. Ella juega con un equipo en un estadio. Necesita ser muy atlética y llevar un casco. Angélica es una chica especial porque casi todos los jugadores son chicos. El deporte favorito de Angélica es

6. Mis amigos y yo llevamos botas especiales para practicar nuestro deporte favorito. Lo practicamos al aire libre en el invierno. Nuestro deporte favorito es

_____ .

UNIDAD 6 Lección 1 Practice Games

Eres... *Repaso de la lección*

Figure out the seven or eight letter word that describes you. You'll find the seven or eight letters by solving the sentence puzzles. Hint: circle all the letters that the two words from **Vocabulario** have in common, and then eliminate those that are also in the third word.

Eres un(a) ____ ____ ____ ____ ____ ____ ____ (____)

1. This letter is in **jugador** and **guante**, but not in **básquetbol**. ____

2. This letter is in **casco** and **bate**, but not in **tenis**. ____

3. This letter is in **ganar** and **nadar**, but not in **jugar**. ____

4. This letter is in **campo** and **pelota**, but not in **equipo**. ____

5. This letter is in **aficionado** and **partido**, but not in **natación**. ____

6. This letter is in **bola** and **fútbol**, but not in **atleta**. ____

7. This letter is in **favorito** and **regla**, but not in **piscina**. ____

8. **FOR GIRLS ONLY:** This letter is in **raqueta** and **cancha**, but not in **voleibol**. ____

¡Saludos! *Práctica de vocabulario*

Tito sent a postcard to his brother about his trip to the beach. He scrambled the letters in some words. Use the clues below the postcard to see what else he did at the beach!

Hola hermanito,

Estoy divirtiéndome (*having fun*). Ayer fui a la yapal a mrota le los. Me puse qeadrobluo
               (1)   (2) (3)   (4)

pero me queme la liep. oL etosin mucho que no pudiste venir conmigo. Mañana voy a
            (5) (6)

creha eqsiu taccouái. También voy a hacer otra cosa. Te voy a dar unas pistas.
(7   )

Con cariño,

Tito

Pistas (*Clues*):

- The word begins with the first letter of the word in number 4.
- The next letter is the third letter of the third word in number 7.
- Next, use the second letter of the third word in number 7.
- Then, use the first letter of the second word in number 3.
- Next use the last letter of the word in number 2.
- Finally, use the last letter of the word in number 1.

_____ _____ _____ _____ _____ _____

1. _____   4. _____   7. _____

2. _____   5. _____

3. _____   6. _____

UNIDAD 6 Lección 2   **Practice Games**

Sopa de letras *Vocabulario en contexto*

Find the eight parts of the body hidden in the word search, then write them on the lines below. Words run horizontally, vertically, and diagonally.

```
S  B  C  A  L  P  E  I  Y  C  Y  X  A  Y
A  R  C  R  I  L  L  O  A  T  C  Ó  H  I
H  A  A  E  C  O  R  T  I  N  O  C  N  C
A  Z  E  S  R  A  Ó  É  L  Z  R  M  Y  T
A  O  E  S  E  C  Q  L  E  R  A  A  É  O
L  S  A  L  T  O  N  A  R  I  Z  C  E  B
P  T  M  U  É  Ó  N  L  T  Y  Ó  R  C  I
E  Y  Ó  R  I  V  M  P  K  R  N  A  H  L
R  O  D  I  L  L  A  A  N  E  É  D  A  L
U  D  P  N  E  H  L  S  G  A  G  I  S  O
E  S  I  E  B  O  E  F  O  O  L  O  O  A
O  R  E  J  A  S  É  R  C  R  C  Ó  F  É
```

1. _____   2. _____

3. _____   4. _____

5. _____   6. _____

7. _____   8. _____

9. _____

¿Qué hicimos? *Práctica de gramática 1*

Write the correct conjugation of the **-ar** verb in the preterite tense in the blanks. Then use the code letters below the answers to form the answer to the question below.

1. Si tenemos que cortar el césped todos los sábados entonces el sábado pasado

   (cortar) ___ ___ ___ ___ ___ ___ el césped.
   　　　　　S　Q　　D　　P　L

2. Si Linda no estaba en clase a tiempo entonces Linda...

   (llegar) ___ ___ ___ ___ tarde.
   　　　　A　　C

3. Si quiero que mis amigos vengan a mi fiesta hoy entonces los

   (invitar) ___ ___ ___ ___ ___ ___ ayer.
   　　　　　K

4. Si tú pasaste el examen de manejar ayer entonces

   (manejar) ___ ___ ___ ___ ___ ___ ___ ___ bien.
   　　　　　E　H　　B　　　J　G　T　U

5. Si usted huele (*smell*) bien hoy entonces usted se (bañar) ___ ___ ___ ___
   anoche.
   　　　　　　　　　　　　　　　　　　　　　　　R　　　F

6. Si hoy quiero usar ropa que no está arrugada (*wrinkled*) entonces

   (planchar) ___ ___ ___ ___ ___ ___ mi ropa ayer.
   　　　　　O　I/M　N

¿Qué hicimos ayer?:

___ ___ ___ ___ ___ ___ ___ ___ ___ ___
A　B　C　D　E　F　G　H　I　J

___ ___ ___ ___ ___ ___ ___ ___ ___ ___
K　L　M　N　　O　P　Q　R　S　T　U

UNIDAD 6 Lección 2

Practice Games

¿Qué se me olvidó? *Gramática en contexto*

Mariana has gone to the beach, but she forgot something. Play the board game to discover what it is.

To play the game: Answer the clues with the correct conjugations of the preterite **-ar** verbs.

⊠ Me (rascar) la cabeza. __ __ __ __ __ __ __

⤢ Se me (olvidar) algo. __ __ __ __ __ __ __

⧗ (Dejar) de pensar en eso. __ __ __ __ __

♎ Y me (acostar) en la arena. __ __ __ __ __ __ __

♋ Una pluma de pájaro cayó en mi cara y (estornudar). __ __ __ __ __ __ __ __ __ __

♏ (Usar) la sombrilla para protegerme del sol. __ __ __

◆ Pero después, la sombrilla se (quebrar). __ __ __ __ __ __ __

❖ (Observar) que se iba a caer. __ __ __ __ __ __ __ __

● Me (levantar) rápido. __ __ __ __ __ __ __ __

♌ Me (bañar) en el agua porque estaba quemada. __ __ __ __ __ __

Start with Empieza and head North. Substitute the symbols with the first letters of the answers above to find out.

_____ __ _____ __ _____ _____

UNIDAD 6 Lección 2

Practice Games

Rimas *Práctica de gramática 2*

Read the following poem. Circle the verbs that have spelling changes in the **yo** form.
Then follow the pattern and complete the poem.

Yo comencé a estar sano,
pero ayer
¡planché un poco mi mano!

Almorcé cinco hamburguesas.
Mi madre tiene razón.
Es mucho para mi corazón.

Pagué cien dólares por la raqueta.
lo malo es,
¡Mi padre no es atleta!

Yo _____ la cuenta
en el restaurante.
¡Una comida para cincuenta!

Crucigrama *Todo junto*

Use the correct forms of the verbs in the preterite tense to complete the sentences and fill in the crossword puzzle.

Horizontal (*across*)

1. Nosotros _____ (terminar) de bucear a las cinco.

3. Vosotros _____ (sacar) muy buenas notas.

5. Yo _____ (jugar) al básquetbol anoche.

7. Tú _____ (nadar) en la piscina de Juan.

Abajo (*down*)

2. Yo _____ (comenzar) de levantar pesas ayer.

4. Los campeones _____ (caminar) en la cancha.

6. Mi hermano _____ (lavar) el perro.

8. Mi madre y mi padre _____ (entrar) a la casa.

Tic-Tac-Toe *Lectura cultural*

Alone or taking turns with a friend, find the forms of the preterite verbs in the boxes to see which letter wins at Tic-Tac-Toe. Place an **X** on the board over the correct answer for number 1. Then allow a partner to place an **O** over number 2. Play until either **X** or **O** appears on the board three times in a row.

X
1. Yo _____ la basura la semana pasada.
3. Ellas _____ la cuenta la última vez.
5. Tú te _____ con el sol.
7. Nosotros _____ en el mar ayer.

O
2. Felipe y tú _____ el pastel de chocolate.
4. Usted no _____ la casa; todavía está sucia.
6. Tú _____ la falda porque estaba arrugada.
8. Yo _____ a caminar a los dos años.

comisteis	limpió	nadamos
empecé	saqué	planchaste
quemaste	podré	pagaron

Who won? _____

UNIDAD 6 Lección 2   Practice Games

Eres... *Repaso de la lección*

Figure out the seven–letter word that says what you don't want to be. You'll find the seven letters by solving the sentence puzzles. Hint: circle all the letters that the two words from Vocabulario have in common, and then eliminate those that are also in the third word.

BOYS: No quieres estar ____ ____ ____ ____ ____ ____ ____

GIRLS: No quieres estar ____ ____ ____ ____ ____ ____ ____

1. This vowel is in **ayer** and **anoche**, but not in **boca**. ____

2. This letter is in **sana** and **nariz**, but not in **rodilla**. ____

3. This letter is in **fuerte** and **enferma**, but not in **piel**. ____

4. This letter is in **esquí** and **herido**, but not in **nariz**. ____

5. This letter is in **mar** and **oreja**, but not in **playa**. ____

6. This letter is in **caminar** and **comenzar**, but not in **corazón**. ____

7. **FOR BOYS ONLY:** This letter is in **sol** and **mano**, but not in **pie**. ____

8. **FOR GIRLS ONLY:** This letter is in **brazo** and **estómago**, but not in **ojo**. ____

Practice Games Answer Key

PAGE 31
Práctica de vocabulario

1. ganar, patinar
2. raqueta, atleta
3. jugador, ganador
4. perder, comprender
5. campo, campeón
6. béisbol, fútbol, básquetbol, voleibol

PAGE 32
Vocabulario en contexto

1. campo
2. pelota
3. estadio
4. bate

EL BÉISBOL

PAGE 33
Práctica de gramática 1

1. juego
2. juegas
3. juega
4. jugamos
5. jugáis
6. juegan

¡No juegues con tu comida!

PAGE 34
Gramática en contexto

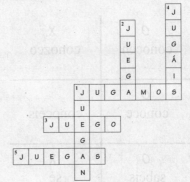

Practice Games Answer Key

PAGE 35
Práctica de gramática 2

X sabemos	O conocen	X conozco
X conoces	O conoce	conocéis
O sabes	O sabéis	X sé

O wins.

PAGE 36
Todo junto

```
        C A N C H A
        F Ú T B O L
  V O L E I B O L
        C A M I S E T A
    E Q U I P O
  C A M P O
        N A T A C I Ó N
        P A T I N E S
  J U G A D O R A
B Á S Q U E T B O L
    T E N I S
```

PAGE 37
Lectura

1. la natación
2. el béisbol
3. el ténis
4. el básquetbol
5. el fútbol americano
6. patinar

PAGE 38
Repaso de la lección

G-A-N-A-D-O-R(-A)

UNIDAD 6 Lección 1
Practice Games Answer Key

Practice Games Answer Key

PAGE 39
Práctica de vocabulario

1. Ayer
2. playa
3. tomar el sol
4. bloquear
5. piel
6. Lo siento
7. hacer esquí acuático

BUCEAR

PAGE 40
Vocabulario en contexto

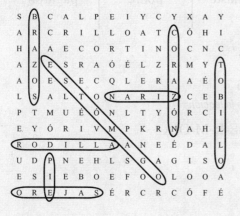

PAGE 41
Práctica de gramática 1

1. cortamos
2. llegó
3. invité
4. manejaste
5. bañó
6. planché

Llegamos a la isla por bote.

PAGE 42
Gramática en contexto

Conjugations: rasqué, olvidó, Dejé, acosté, estornudé, Usé, quebró, Observé, levanté, bañé

bloqueador

PAGE 43
Práctica de gramática 2

Circled words:
comencé
Almorcé
Pagué

Yo **pagué** la cuenta en el restaurante.

Practice Games Answer Key

PAGE 44

Todo junto

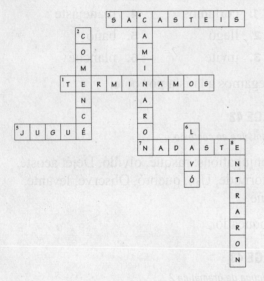

PAGE 45

Lectura cultural

O comisteis	O limpió	X nadamos
O empecé	X saqué	O planchaste
X quemaste	O podré	X pagaron

X wins.

PAGE 46

Repaso de la lección

E–N–F–E–R–M-O/A

UNIDAD 6 Lección 2

Practice Games Answer Key

Video Activities *Vocabulario*

PRE-VIEWING ACTIVITY

Answer the questions about sports.

1 What is your favorite sport?

_____

2 What equipment do you use in your favorite sport?

_____

3 Where do you play your favorite sport?

_____

4 What sports do you enjoy watching?

_____

VIEWING ACTIVITY

Read the items before you watch the video. While you watch, indicate with a checkmark (🕐) whether the games involve each item. Some of the items are involved in more than one game.

béisbòl	voleibol	tenis	
_____	_____	_____	una pelota
_____	_____	_____	los jugadores
_____	_____	_____	un bate
_____	_____	_____	una raqueta
_____	_____	_____	las reglas
_____	_____	_____	un partido
_____	_____	_____	un guante
_____	_____	_____	un(a) ganador(a)
_____	_____	_____	un casco

Video Activities *Vocabulario*

POST-VIEWING ACTIVITY

After you watch the video, indicate whether each item is true (T) or false (F).

1. Fernando está en el equipo rojo.   T   F

2. El béisbol es el deporte favorito de Isabel.   T   F

3. Fernando lleva un guante para jugar al tennis.   T   F

4. El equipo azúl gana el partido de béisbol.   T   F

5. Los aficionados miran el partido de básquetbol.   T   F

6. Fernando e Isabel comprenden las reglas del
   fútbol americano.   T   F

7. Isabel juega al tenis con una raqueta.   T   F

UNIDAD 6 Lección 1

Video Activities

Video Activities *Telehistoria escena 1*

PRE-VIEWING ACTIVITY

Answer the following questions about sports.

1 Do you or any of your friends play any sports?

_____

2 Which sports do you and/or your friends play?

_____

3 When was the last time that you or your friends' team won a game? What was the score?

_____

4 When was the last time that you or your friends' team lost a game? What was the score?

_____

VIEWING ACTIVITY

Read the following list of sports before watching the video. Then, while watching the video, check off (🕐) the sports that Mario's brother *likes*.

_____ el voleibol

_____ patinar en línea

_____ el tenis

_____ fútbol americano

_____ nadar

_____ el fútbol

_____ el béisbol

_____ el básquetbol

Video Activities *Telehistoria escena 1*

POST-VIEWING ACTIVITY

Choose the correct word(s) to complete each sentence.

1. Isabel dice que su equipo siempre _____ .

   a. gana

   b. pierde

2. Mario piensa que Isabel es una jugadora de béisbol muy _____ .

   a. buena

   b. mala

3. Mario dice que su equipo va a ser _____ hoy.

   a. los aficionados

   b. los campeones

4. Mario no puede ir al café con Isabel porque tiene que _____ .

   a. pasar un rato con su hermano

   b. ir de compras

5. El hermano de Mario es _____ .

   a. perezoso

   b. atlético

6. Su hermano ya tiene un bate y _____ .

   a. un casco

   b. una pelota de béisbol

7. Mario no quiere comprar patines en línea porque _____ .

   a. cuestan mucho dinero

   b. su hermano ya tiene unos

8. Al hermano de Mario le gusta _____ .

   a. la natación

   b. el fútbol americano

UNIDAD 6 Lección 1

Video Activities

Unidad 6, Lección 1
Video Activities

54

¡Avancemos! 1
Unit Resource Book

Video Activities *Telehistoria escena 2*

PRE-VIEWING ACTIVITY

Answer the following questions.

1 List five different sports and the equipment needed to play each sport.

sport: equipment:

_____   _____

_____   _____

_____   _____

_____   _____

_____   _____

2 Which, if any, of the sports listed above do you play?

_____

3 Would you consider this an expensive sport to play?

_____

VIEWING ACTIVITY

Read the list of sports equipment below before watching the video. Then, while you watch the video, indicate with a checkmark (☺) whether Mario or Isabel is interested in each piece of equipment for him or herself. Hint: There are some items that neither of them is interested in.

Mario	Isabel	
_____	_____	la bola de fútbol
_____	_____	la pelota de tenis
_____	_____	la raqueta
_____	_____	la bola de voleibol
_____	_____	la bola de básquetbol
_____	_____	el casco
_____	_____	el guante de béisbol

UNIDAD 6 Lección 1 Video Activities

Video Activities *Telehistoria escena 2*

POST-VIEWING ACTIVITY

Indicate if each of the following statements is T for true or F for false.

1. Isabel piensa que el guante de béisbol es un buen regalo.   T   F

2. A Mario le gusta la raqueta.   T   F

3. Mario no piensa que una bola de básquetbol es un buen regalo para su hermano.   T   F

4. No es el cumpleaños de Isabel.   T   F

5. El hermano de Mario necesita un casco.   T   F

6. Mario quiere llevar un casco cuando juega al tenis.   T   F

7. Isabel dice que jugar al tenis es peligroso.   T   F

8. Isabel juega mucho al tenis.   T   F

9. A Isabel le gusta jugar al voleibol.   T   F

10. Mario no sabe todavía que va a comprar para su hermano.   T   F

UNIDAD 6 Lección 1

Video Activities

Video Activities *Telehistoria escena 3*

PRE-VIEWING ACTIVITY

Answer the following questions.

1 When was the last time you bought a present for a friend?

_____

2 Do you ever have a hard time finding the right gift for someone?

_____

3 What do you do if you can't find a present your friend will like?

_____

4 Have you ever bought a present for a friend that he or she didn't like?

_____

VIEWING ACTIVITY

Read the sentences below before watching the video. Then, while you watch the video, indicate with a checkmark (⏱) if you hear each of the following sentences.

_____ ¡Es la camiseta de Alicia!

_____ Ella está aquí, en Santo Domingo.

_____ Trini es su jugadora de fútbol favorito.

_____ ¡Tú debes encontrar a Trini!

_____ Trini Salgado va a estar en el estadio hoy a las seis de la tarde.

_____ Los primeros diez aficionados pueden tener su autógrafo en una pelota de béisbol o en una camiseta.

_____ ¿A tu hermano le gusta Trini Salgado?

Video Activities *Telehistoria escena 3*

POST-VIEWING ACTIVITY

Circle the verb that best completes each sentence.

1. Isabel conoce / sabe a Trini.

2. Isabel conoce / sabe que Trini está en Santo Domingo.

3. Alicia no conoce / sabe a Trini Salgado.

4. Mario y Isabel no conocen / saben donde encontrar Trini Salgado.

5. Los primeros cien aficionados en el estadio pueden conocer / saber a Trini.

6. Después de comprar la camiseta Mario y Isabel van a conocer / saber a Trini.

7. Mario no conoce / sabe si a su hermano le gusta Trini Salgado.

UNIDAD 6 Lección 1

Video Activities

Video Activities *Vocabulario*

PRE-VIEWING ACTIVITY

Answer the following questions about the beach.

1 If you could go to the beach today, what would you like to do there?

_____

2 Why is it necessary to protect yourself from the sun when you are at the beach?

_____

3 How can you protect yourself from the sun when you are at the beach?

_____

4 Name two activities that are fun to do at the beach. Why are these activities fun?

_____

VIEWING ACTIVITY

Read the activities below before watching the video. While you watch, write **sí** (*yes*) next to the activities that Isabel and Fernando do at the beach. Write **no** (*no*) next to the activities that they do not do there.

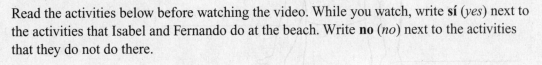

_____ **1.** caminar

_____ **2.** jugar al voleibol

_____ **3.** nadar en el mar

_____ **4.** poner bloqueador de sol

_____ **5.** comer helado

_____ **6.** tomar el sol

_____ **7.** ver el mar

UNIDAD 6 Lección 2   Video Activities

Video Activities *Vocabulario*

POST-VIEWING ACTIVITY

After you watch the video, label the picture of the boy. Use the words in the word bank.

boca	brazos	manos	nariz	ojos
orejas	piernas	tobillos	pies	

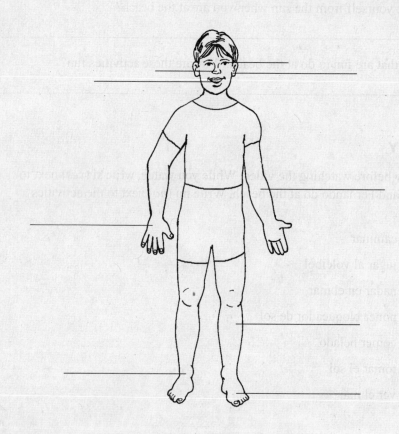

UNIDAD 6 Lección 2

Video Activities

60 Unidad 6, Lección 2
Video Activities

¡Avancemos! 1
Unit Resource Book

Copyright © by McDougal Littell, a division of Houghton Mifflin Company.

Video Activities *Telehistoria escena 1*

PRE-VIEWING ACTIVITY

Answer the following questions.

1 When was the last time you seriously injured yourself?

_____

2 What did you injure?

_____

3 When was the last time you were sick?

_____

4 What was the illness?

_____

5 What were your symptoms?

_____

VIEWING ACTIVITY

Read the parts of the body below before watching the video. Then, while watching the video, indicate with a checkmark (🕐) which parts of the body are mentioned by Mario or Isabel.

_____	la boca	_____	la oreja
_____	el brazo	_____	el pie
_____	la cabeza	_____	el corazón
_____	la piel	_____	la pierna
_____	el cuerpo	_____	la rodilla
_____	el estómago	_____	el tobillo
_____	la mano	_____	el ojo
_____	la nariz		

Video Activities *Telehistoria escena 1*

POST-VIEWING ACTIVITY

How would Mario respond to each of Isabel's statements or questions? Choose the most appropriate answer to each question or statement.

1. _____ ¿Sabes montar en bicicleta?

2. _____ ¡Hay que llevar un casco!

3. _____ ¿Estás bien?

4. _____ ¿Qué te pasa con la boca?

5. _____ No debes caminar.

a. Ay, sí. Aquí lo tengo.

b. Sí. Soy fuerte y sano.

c. Ya sé, pero tenemos que ser los primeros aficionados en el estadio.

d. Claro. Es fácil.

e. Nada, pero me duele un poco el pie.

Video Activities *Telehistoria escena 2*

PRE-VIEWING ACTIVITY

Answer the following questions.

1 Have you or a friend ever broken or seriously injured anything? _____

2 What did you or your friend hurt or break?

_____

3 Describe in a short paragraph how the injury happened.

_____

_____

_____

VIEWING ACTIVITY

Read the phrases below before watching the video. Then, while you watch the video, indicate with a checkmark (🕐) whether Isabel, la doctora (*the doctor*), or Mario say each phrase.

Isabel	la doctora	Mario	
____	____	____	Lo hice bien por un rato.
____	____	____	Ahora estoy herido.
____	____	____	Montó en su bicicleta.
____	____	____	¿Qué hiciste?
____	____	____	¿Está usted enfermo?
____	____	____	¿Sabe, está en el estadio hoy?
____	____	____	Le duelen la pierna y la cabeza.
____	____	____	No más bicicletas, ¡por favor!
____	____	____	¡El señor de las frutas caminó delante de mi bicicleta!
____	____	____	Lo ayudé a caminar.

Video Activities *Telehistoria escena 2*

POST-VIEWING ACTIVITY

According to the video, put the following events in the correct order.

_____ Isabel y Mario buscaron a Trini Salgado para pedir su autógrafo.

_____ Un señor caminó delante de Mario.

_____ Mario intentó andar pero Isabel necesitó ayudar a Mario a caminar.

_____ Mario compró una camiseta para su hermano.

_____ Mario bajó por la calle.

_____ Isabel y Mario montaron en sus bicicletas.

UNIDAD 6 Lección 2

Video Activities

Unidad 6, Lección 2
Video Activities

64

¡Avancemos! 1
Unit Resource Book

Video Activities *Telehistoria escena 3*

PRE-VIEWING ACTIVITY

❶ Answer the following questions about your health.

1. List five activities that are good for your health.

_____

_____

2. How often do you do the activities listed in number one?

_____

_____

3. Do you consider yourself to be in shape or healthy?

_____

4. What are two things you could do to be a healthier person?

_____

_____

VIEWING ACTIVITY

❷ Read the following sentences before watching the video. Than, while you watch the video, indicate if each of the following statements are T for true or F for false.

1. A Mario le duele la rodilla.　　　　　　　T　　F

2. Mario no puede jugar al fútbol ni al béisbol
por cuatro semanas.　　　　　　　　　　T　　F

3. La doctora dice que Mario no puede
levantar pesas.　　　　　　　　　　　　　T　　F

4. Mario no tiene dinero para pagar la doctora.　T　　F

5. Isabel y Mario van a bucear mañana.　　　　T　　F

6. Mario va a traer el bloqueador de sol.　　　　T　　F

Video Activities *Telehistoria escena 3*

POST-VIEWING ACTIVITY

Choose the word(s) that best complete(s) each of the following sentences.

la playa	herido	un tobillo	el agua
tomar el sol	los brazos	bloqueador de sol	el mar

1. Mario puede levantar pesas con _____ .

2. Mario pagó la camiseta y _____ .

3. Todavía Mario está _____ .

4. Isabel y Mario piensan ir a _____ .

5. Isabel dice que _____ es bueno para los enfermos.

6. Mario jugó una vez con _____ herido.

7. Isabel quiere _____ en la playa.

8. Mario piensa que no necesita _____ porque tomó el sol por 15 años.

UNIDAD 6 Lección 2

Video Activities

Video Activities Answer Key

VOCABULARIO pp. 51–52

PRE-VIEWING ACTIVITY

1. Answers will vary. Possible answer: My favorite sport is baseball.
2. Answers will vary. Possible answer: I use a ball, a bat and a glove.
3. Answers will vary. Possible answer: I play baseball on a baseball diamond.
4. Answers will vary. Possible answer: I like watching basketball and football.

VIEWING ACTIVITY

una pelota: béisbol, voleibol, tenis

los jugadores: béisbol, voleibol, tenis

un bate: béisbol

una raqueta: tenis

las reglas: béisbol, voleibol, tenis

un partido: béisbol, voleibol, tenis

un guante: béisbol

un(a) ganador(a): béisbol, voleibol, tenis

un casco: béisbol

POST-VIEWING ACTIVITY

1. F
2. T
3. F
4. F
5. T
6. F
7. T

TELEHISTORIA ESCENA 1 pp. 53–54

PRE-VIEWING ACTIVITY

1. Answers will vary. Possible answer: Yes, I play sports.
2. Answers will vary. Possible answer: I play baseball on the school team.
3. Answers will vary. Possible answer: Our baseball team won last week's game 7 to 0.
4. Answers will vary. Possible answer: Our baseball team lost our last game. The score was 12 to 6.

VIEWING ACTIVITY

Checked items should be: patinar en línea; nadar; el béisbol

POST-VIEWING ACTIVITY

1. a
2. a
3. b
4. b
5. b
6. b
7. a
8. a

TELEHISTORIA ESCENA 2 pp. 55–56

PRE-VIEWING ACTIVITY

1. Answers will vary. Possible answer: 1. basketball: basketball, high-top sports shoes 2. tennis: tennis balls, tennis racket, good tennis shoes 3. soccer: rebounder net, soccer ball 4. baseball: helmet, glove, bat, baseball 5. snowboarding: wrist guards, knee guards, snowboard, goggles, snow suit, snow boots
2. Answers will vary. Possible answer: I snowboard.
3. Answers will vary. Possible answer: It is very expensive!

VIEWING ACTIVITY

Mario: el casco

Isabel: la raqueta; la bola de básquetbol

POST-VIEWING ACTIVITY

1. T
2. F
3. T
4. T
5. F
6. T
7. F
8. F
9. T
10. T

TELEHISTORIA ESCENA 3 pp. 57–58

PRE-VIEWING ACTIVITY

1. Answers will vary. Possible answer: I bought my friend Luis a present on his birthday.
2. Answers will vary. Possible answer: Yes, I sometimes can't think of the right gift for someone.
3. Answers will vary. Possible answer: I usually buy him or her something that I know I would like to have as a present.
4. Answers will vary. Possible answer: No, not that I am aware of!

VIEWING ACTIVITY

Checked items should be: Ella está aquí, en Santo Domingo. Trini Salgado va a estar en el estadio hoy a las seis de la tarde. ¿A tu hermano le gusta Trini Salgado?

POST-VIEWING ACTIVITY

1. conoce
2. sabe
3. conoce
4. saben
5. conocer
6. conocer
7. sabe

VOCABULARIO pp. 59–60

PRE-VIEWING ACTIVITY

1. Answers will vary. Possible answer: I would like to swim, walk around, and sunbathe.
2. Answers will vary. Possible answer: I get sunburned and it hurts.
3. Answers will vary. Possible answer: I put sunscreen on my nose, cheeks, arms, and legs.
4. Answers will vary. Possible answer: Swimming and sunbathing. They're fun because they're relaxing.

VIEWING ACTIVITY

1. sí
2. no
3. no
4. sí
5. no
6. sí
7. sí

POST-VIEWING ACTIVITY

mouth: boca; arms: brazos; hands: manos; nose: nariz; eyes: ojos; ears: orejas; legs: piernas; ankles: tobillos; feet: pies

UNIDAD 6 Video Activities Answer Key

Video Activities Answer Key

TELEHISTORIA ESCENA 1 pp. 61–62

PRE-VIEWING ACTIVITY

1. Answers will vary. Possible answer: I seriously injured myself one year ago.

2. Answers will vary. Possible answer: I broke my wrist when I fell off my bike.

3. Answers will vary. Possible answer: I was really sick in January.

4. Answers will vary. Possible answer: I had the flu.

5. Answers will vary. Possible answer: I had a sore throat, an achy back, a really bad headache, and a fever.

VIEWING ACTIVITY

Checked items should be: la boca; la cabeza; la piel; la nariz; el pie; la pierna; el tobillo

POST-VIEWING ACTIVITY

1. d
2. a
3. b
4. e
5. c

TELEHISTORIA ESCENA 2 pp. 63–64

PRE-VIEWING ACTIVITY

1. Answers will vary. Possible answer: Yes.

2. Answers will vary. Possible answer: I knocked out my front teeth.

3. Answers will vary. Possible answer: I was snowboarding when I hit a rock on the slope and lost control. My snowboard flew out from under me and hit me in the face. The board knocked out my front teeth.

VIEWING ACTIVITY

Isabel: Montó en su bicicleta. Le duelen la pierna y la cabeza. Lo ayudé a caminar.

la doctora: ¿Qué hiciste? ¿Está usted enfermo? No más bicicletas, ¡por favor!

Mario: Lo hice bien por un rato. Ahora estoy herido. ¿Sabe si está en el estadio hoy? ¡El señor de las frutas caminó delante de mi bicicleta!

POST-VIEWING ACTIVITY

Isabel y Mario buscaron a Trini Salgado para pedir su autógrafo. **2**

Un señor caminó delante de Mario. **5**

Mario intentó andar pero Isabel necesitó ayudarlo a Mario a caminar. **6**

Mario compró una camiseta para su hermano. **1**

Mario bajó por la calle. **4**

Isabel y Mario montaron en sus bicicletas. **3**

TELEHISTORIA ESCENA 3 pp. 65–66

PRE-VIEWING ACTIVITY

1. Answers will vary. Possible answer: riding a bike, eating low-fat foods, not eating fast food, jogging, drinking eight glasses of water a day

2. Answers will vary. Possible answer: I ride my bike once a week. I always eat low-fat foods. I never jog nor do I drink eight glasses of water a day. I only eat fast food on weekends.

3. Answers will vary. Possible answer: I am in shape and healthy.

4. Answers will vary. Possible answer: I could drink more water every day and work out more often.

VIEWING ACTIVITY

1. T
2. T
3. F
4. T
5. F
6. T

POST-VIEWING ACTIVITY

1. los brazos
2. el agua
3. herido
4. la playa
5. el mar
6. un tobillo
7. tomar el sol
8. bloqueador de sol

Video Scripts

VOCABULARIO

Isabel: Hola. Me llamo Isabel.

Mario: Y yo soy Mario.

Juntos: ¿Quieres practicar deportes?

Mario: Yo soy un jugador. Él también es un jugador y ella es una jugadora. Todos somos atletas. Y somos un equipo. El equipo Azul.

Isabel: Mi equipo es el equipo Rojo. Y aquí está el campo de béisbol.

Mario: Vamos a jugar un partido de béisbol.

Isabel: ¡Mi deporte favorito!

Mario: La pelota.

Isabel: El bate.

Mario: El guante.

Isabel: Y… el casco.

Kids: ¡Campeona! ¡Campeona! ¡Campeona!

Isabel: ¡Mi equipo gana!

Mario: ¡Y mi equipo pierde!

Isabel: ¿No te gusta el béisbol? Puedes jugar al básquetbol.

Isabel: Estamos en una cancha de básquetbol… ¡Soy la ganadora! Mira, los aficionados.

Mario: ¿No te gusta el básquetbol? Puedes jugar al fútbol americano. ¿Comprendes las reglas?

Isabel: Con la bola puedes jugar al tenis. Una raqueta.

Mario: Me gusta más jugar al voleibol.

Mario: ¡Somos unos atletas muy buenos!

Isabel: Sí.

TELEHISTORIA ESCENA 1

Isabel: Hoy tu equipo va a perder el partido, Mario. Mi equipo siempre gana.

Mario: Sí, Isabel. Eres muy buena jugadora de béisbol. Pero hoy nosotros vamos a ser los campeones.

Isabel: ¿Qué vas a hacer después de la escuela las clases? ¿Vamos al café? ¡El ganador no paga!

Mario: No puedo. Tengo que comprar un regalo. Es el cumpleaños de mi hermano.

Isabel: ¿Qué vas a comprar? Es un atleta. Le gusta el béisbol, ¿no?

Mario: Sí, pero tiene un bate y pelotas de béisbol.

Isabel: ¿Le gusta patinar en línea?

Mario: Sí, pero los patines en línea cuestan mucho dinero.

Isabel: ¿Le gusta el fútbol americano? ¿Y el tenis? La natación, ¿le gusta?

Mario: Sí, le gusta nadar pero, ¿qué le puedo comprar? ¿Una piscina? ¿Agua?

Video Scripts

TELEHISTORIA ESCENA 2

Isabel: Un guante de béisbol. Me gusta para tu hermano. Me gusta la raqueta.

Mario: No, una bola de básquetbol no. Es un regalo para mi hermano; no es tu cumpleaños.

Isabel: ¿Necesita un casco?

Mario: No, pero yo necesito un casco para jugar al tenis.

Isabel: ¡Un partido de tenis no es peligroso!

Mario: Tú no juegas al tenis con mi hermano.

Isabel: No, no juego al tenis. Pero me gusta el voleibol. ¿Tu hermano juega al voleibol?

TELEHISTORIA ESCENA 3

Mario: ¡Es como la camiseta de Alicia!

Isabel: ¿Tu amiga de Miami?

Mario: Sí. ¿Conoces a Trini Salgado? Ella está aquí, en Santo Domingo.

Isabel: Lo sé. ¿Alicia la conoce?

Mario: No, pero Trini es su jugadora de fútbol favorita. Alicia quiere un autógrafo en la camiseta. Y yo debo encontrar a Trini…

Vendedor: ¿Buscan a Trini Salgado? ¿Saben dónde encontrar a Trini Salgado?

Radio: La jugadora de fútbol Trini Salgado va a estar en el estadio hoy a las seis de la tarde. Los primeros quinientos aficionados pueden conocer a Trini. Y los primeros cien aficionados pueden tener su autógrafo en una bola de fútbol o en una camiseta.

Mario: ¡Vamos!

Isabel: ¿Y el regalo de tu hermano? ¿A tu hermano…le gusta Trini Salgado?

Mario: No sé. ¡Pero sé que le gustan las camisetas con autógrafos de atletas importantes!

Video Scripts

VOCABULARIO

Mario: ¡Hola! Estamos en la playa. Nos gusta mucho caminar y ver el mar.

Isabel: Mario y yo estamos sanos.

Mario: Yo soy muy fuerte porque levanto pesas.

Isabel: Nos gusta tomar el sol. Ah, pero debemos usar bloqueador de sol.

Isabel: ¡No, no, no! ¿Quieres tener la piel roja? Debes usar más bloqueador de sol. En la nariz… en las orejas… aquí, por los ojos y la boca.

Mario: No, en la boca no!

Isabel: Lo siento.

Mario: ¿En los brazos y las manos?

Isabel: Sí. En las piernas, en las rodillas, en los tobillos, y en los pies.

Mario: No, ¡en los pies no!

Isabel: Lo siento. ¿Estás herido?

Mario: No.

Mario: ¡Ayyyyyy!

Isabel: ¡Mario! ¿Estás enfermo? ¿Te duele la cabeza?

Mario: No. Me duelen los pies.

Isabel: Vamos a casa.

TELEHISTORIA ESCENA 1

Isabel: Estamos cerca del estadio. ¿Por qué vamos en bicicleta?

Mario: ¡Tenemos que ser los primeros aficionados en el estadio!

Isabel: Mario, ¿sabes montar en bicicleta?

Mario: Sí, sí, ¡es fácil!

Isabel: ¡Necesitas el casco!

Isabel: ¿Qué hiciste?

Mario: ¡No estoy herido!

Isabel: Pero, ¿y el tobillo? ¿y la pierna?

Mario: Soy fuerte y sano…

Isabel: ¿Y la cabeza? ¡Mario! ¡Tienes la piel muy roja! ¡La nariz! Abre la boca. ¿Puedes caminar?

Mario: Sí. Me duele un poco el pie… pero puedo caminar. ¡Vamos, es tarde!

Isabel: No, no debes caminar.

Mario: Pero… ¿Y Trini Salgado?

Isabel: ¿Trini Salgado? ¡Un autógrafo no es importante! ¡Vamos! Lo siento.

TELEHISTORIA ESCENA 2

Doctora: ¿Mario Álvarez? ¿Está usted enfermo?

Mario: No, no, voy a casa.

Isabel: Le duelen la pierna y la cabeza. Lo ayudé a caminar.

Doctora: ¿Qué hiciste?

Isabel: Pues, montó en su bicicleta… ¡cerca de unas frutas!

Mario: Compré una camiseta para mi hermano. Isabel y yo buscamos a Trini Salgado para pedir un autógrafo. ¿Sabe que ella está en el estadio hoy? Monté en mi bicicleta, y bajé por la calle…

Doctora: ¿Llevaste un casco?

Isabel: Sí, ¡pero Mario piensa que es Lance Armstrong!

Mario: Isabel, ¡el señor de las frutas caminó delante de mi bicicleta!

Isabel: Y allí… ¡Púm!

Doctora: Mario, ¿sabes montar en bicicleta?

Video Scripts

Mario: Mmmm, Sí, es fácil... Monté bien por un rato...

Doctora: ¿Te gustó?

Mario: Sí. Ahora estoy herido, pero, ¡me gustó!

Doctora: Por la salud de tu amigo... No más bicicletas, ¡por favor!

TELEHISTORIA ESCENA 3

Doctora: El tobillo está bien. ¿Te duele la rodilla?

Mario: No. No. Un poco.

Doctora: No puedes jugar al fútbol, y no puedes jugar al béisbol por cuatro semanas.

Mario: ¿Puedo levantar pesas?

Doctora: Levantar pesas, sí. Pero con los brazos, con las piernas no.

Isabel: Muchas gracias, doctora. Adiós.

Mario: ¿Puedes pagar? Yo pagué la camiseta y el agua. ¡Ay! El autógrafo para Alicia... Comencé a...

Isabel: Sí, Mario! ¡Lo siento! Comenzaste a buscar a Trini, pero, ¿qué podemos hacer? Estás herido. ¿Vamos a la playa mañana? El mar es bueno para los enfermos.

Mario: ¡No estoy enfermo! Una vez jugué al fútbol con el tobillo herido.

Isabel: Podemos tomar el sol. Traigo el bloqueador de sol.

Mario: ¿Qué? ¡No, no! Tomé el sol por 15 años, no necesito bloqueador de sol. ¡Soy fuerte y sano!

Mario: Yo traigo el bloqueador de sol.

COMPARACIÓN CULTURAL VIDEO

If you want to stay healthy, besides eating a healthy diet, you should practice a sport. Sports will make you stronger and will keep your heart beating strong. Here we are going to show you the number one sport in the Dominican Republic, a park in Puerto Rico where people go to exercise, and an adventurous way to get outside and play in Costa Rica.

In most Spanish–speaking countries soccer is a hugely popular sport. Kids and adults play it all the time: in the streets, in the park, and even at the beach.

Dominican Republic
But in the Dominican Republic, the biggest sport is baseball. Dominicans are so good at it that many are recruited to come to the United States and play in the Major Leagues.

Puerto Rico
In Puerto Rico, just like in other Caribbean countries, basketball is a very popular sport. Kids enjoy getting together with friends to play almost every day. But you don't need a team sport to keep healthy. In Puerto Rico people also go to Central Park to jog or play tennis.

This is Escambron Beach on the northern coast of Puerto Rico. Here you can practice surfing, or you can swim...with the sharks. This is definitely a very adventurous sport, but not as exciting as...

Costa Rica
...bungee jumping! In Costa Rica this sport has become very popular. It is a way to enjoy nature and to definitely raise your heart rate. When practiced with all safety measures in place, this can also be a good way of getting out and enjoying a VERY active lifestyle.

It is very important to participate in sports, and there are a lot of different sports to choose from. Get an idea from Dominican kids who play baseball to perfection, or Puerto Ricans who make exercise a part of their daily life. Even if you decide to jump from a bridge like kids in Costa Rica, be safe, have fun and keep moving!!

Audio Scripts

PRESENTACIÓN DE VOCABULARIO

Level 1 Textbook pp. 302-303

Level 1B Textbook pp. 104-106

TXT CD 6, Track 1

A. ¡Hola! Me llamo Mario. Soy atleta y mi deporte favorito es el béisbol. Hoy tenemos un partido con el equipo rojo.

B. Acabamos de perder el partido, cuatro a cinco. Mi amiga Isabel y su equipo son los ganadores. Tal vez debo practicar otro deporte.

C. Me gusta nadar, pero la piscina está lejos de mi casa. El voleibol es divertido, pero prefiero el béisbol.

D. De vez en cuando voy al campo para jugar al fútbol americano, pero es difícil comprender las reglas. Me gusta el básquetbol, pero nunca gano. También voy a la cancha de tenis, pero siempre hay muchas personas allí. Puedo patinar en línea, pero es peligroso. ¡Es mejor jugar al béisbol!

En la República Dominicana se dice…

In the Dominican Republic the word for baseball game is el juego de pelota.

¡A RESPONDER!

Level 1 Textbook p. 303

TXT CD 6, Track 2

Level 1B Textbook p. 106

Level 1B TXT CD 1, Track 16

Escucha la lista de palabras asociadas con los deportes. Si es una palabra que asocias con el béisbol, levanta la mano.

1. la raqueta
2. el guante
3. la pelota
4. los patines en línea
5. el bate
6. la piscina
7. el casco
8. el campo

TELEHISTORIA ESCENA 1

Level 1 Textbook p. 305

Level 1B Textbook p. 108

TXT CD 6, Track 3

Isabel: Hoy tu equipo va a perder el partido, Mario. Mi equipo siempre gana.

Mario: Sí, Isabel, eres muy buena jugadora de béisbol. Pero hoy nosotros vamos a ser los campeones.

Isabel: ¿Qué vas a hacer después de las clases? ¿Vamos al café?

Mario: Tengo que comprar un regalo. Es el cumpleaños de mi hermano.

Isabel: ¿Qué vas a comprar? Es un atleta. Le gusta el béisbol, ¿no?

Mario: Sí, pero tiene un bate y pelotas de béisbol.

Isabel: ¿Le gusta patinar en línea?

Mario: Sí, pero los patines en línea cuestan mucho dinero.

Isabel: ¿Le gusta el fútbol americano? ¿El tenis? La natación, ¿le gusta?

Mario: Sí, le gusta nadar pero, ¿qué puedo comprar? ¿Una piscina? ¿Agua?

ACTIVIDAD 6 - ¿A QUÉ JUEGAN?

Level 1 Textbook p. 308

TXT CD 6, Track 4

Level 1B Textbook p. 111

Level 1B TXT CD, Track 17

Estos atletas hablan de los lugares donde juegan. Escucha las descripciones y escribe a qué juegan estas personas.

Elena: Hola, soy Elena. Soy jugadora de fútbol. Es mi deporte favorito. Juego todos los días en el campo.

Rogelio: Me llamo Rogelio. Mi amigo José y yo jugamos en la cancha de voleibol.

Sr. Morales: Pero, ¿dónde están los bates y los guantes? Hoy el equipo juega en el campo de béisbol…

Elena: Señor Morales, ¿qué hacen los maestros después de las clases?

Sr. Morales: Jugamos en la cancha de básquetbol. Tenemos un partido a las cinco.

Rogelio: Tomás, ¿a qué juegas?

Tomás: Soy jugador de fútbol americano… Juego todas las tardes en el campo de la escuela.

Atleta profesional: Soy atleta profesional. Tengo mi raqueta de tenis y pelotas… juego en la cancha cerca de mi casa.

TELEHISTORIA ESCENA 2

Level 1 Textbook p. 310

Level 1B Textbook p. 114

TXT CD 6, Track 5

Isabel: Un guante de béisbol. Me gusta para tu hermano.

Isabel: Me gusta la raqueta.

Mario: No, una bola de básquetbol, no. Es un regalo para mi hermano; no es tu cumpleaños.

Isabel: ¿Necesita un casco?

Mario: No, pero necesito un casco para jugar al tenis.

Isabel: ¡Un partido de tenis no es peligroso!

Mario: Tú no juegas al tenis con mi hermano.

Isabel: No, no juego al tenis. Pero me gusta el voleibol. ¿Tu hermano juega al voleibol?

PRONUNCIACIÓN

Level 1 Textbook p. 311

Level 1B Textbook p. 115

TXT CD 6, Track 6

La letra **g** con **a, o, u**

Before **a, o, u**, and consonants, the Spanish **g** is pronounced like the g in the English word game.

Listen and repeat.

Audio Scripts

ga

ganar

go

tengo

gu

guante

g + consonant

reglas

A Gregorio le gusta jugar al béisbol en agosto.

TELEHISTORIA COMPLETA

Level 1 Textbook p. 315

Level 1B Textbook p. 120

TXT CD 6, Track 7

Escena 1 - Resumen

En un partido de béisbol, Mario habla con Isabel. Él tiene que comprar un regalo para el cumpleaños de su hermano.

Escena 2 - Resumen

Isabel y Mario buscan un regalo en una tienda de deportes. Mario no sabe qué va a comprar.

Escena 3

Mario: ¡Es como la camiseta de Alicia! ¿Conoces a Trini Salgado? Ella está aquí, en Santo Domingo.

Isabel: Lo sé. ¿Alicia la conoce?

Mario: No, pero Trini es su jugadora de fútbol favorita. Alicia quiere un autógrafo en la camiseta. Y yo debo encontrar a Trini…

Vendedor: ¿Buscan a Trini Salgado? ¿Saben dónde encontrar a Trini Salgado?

Radio: La jugadora de fútbol Trini Salgado va a estar en el estadio hoy a las seis de la tarde. Los primeros quinientos aficionados pueden conocer a Trini.

Mario: ¡Vamos!

Isabel: ¿A tu hermano le gusta Trini Salgado?

Mario: No sé. ¡Pero sé que le gustan las camisetas con autógrafos de atletas importantes!

ACTIVIDAD 19 (22) - INTEGRACIÓN

Level 1 Textbook p. 317

TXT CD 6, Track 8

Level 1B Textbook p. 122

Level 1B TXT CD 1, Track 18

Lee el anuncio de un partido y escucha a los comentaristas. Luego di qué equipo va a ganar y por qué.

FUENTE 2

TXT CD 6, Track 9

Level 1B TXT CD 1, Track 19

¿Cómo juegan los equipos?

¿Cómo practican antes de los partidos?

Antonio: Buenas tardes. Aquí estamos en el Centro de Deportes Solimar. Soy Antonio y les presento a mi compañera, Rosa.

Rosa: Gracias, Antonio. Hoy juegan dos equipos muy buenos: Los Cometas y Los Pumas.

Antonio: Es cierto. Conozco a Los Cometas. Los jugadores siempre vienen a la cancha muy tranquilos porque saben practicar muy bien antes del partido. Practican todos los días y son muy serios.

Rosa: Hmmm... tienes razón. Los Pumas saben jugar pero no saben practicar bien antes de los partidos. No practican, no comen bien y no duermen. Ya están cansados antes de empezar a jugar.

Antonio: Bueno, ahora los dos equipos están en la cancha...

LECTURA: UN CLUB DE DEPORTES

Level 1 Textbook pp. 318-319

Level 1B Textbook pp. 124-125

TXT CD 6, Track 10

This is a brochure for a sports club in Santo Domingo.

Palacio de los Deportes.

¿Eres atlético? ¿Te gusta practicar deportes? Si la respuesta es sí, ven al Palacio de los Deportes.

¿Te gusta nadar? Tenemos una piscina olímpica.

¿Te gusta jugar al tenis? Tenemos cinco canchas de tenis.

¿Te gusta jugar al béisbol? Tenemos un campo de béisbol.

¿Te gusta jugar al básquetbol? Tenemos dos canchas de básquetbol.

¿Quieres comer después de jugar? Tenemos un café que sirve comidas y bebidas ricas y nutritivas.

Para nuestros socios

Si no sabes practicar los siguientes deportes, tenemos clases de natación, tenis, artes marciales, ejercicios aeróbicos.

Si quieres jugar con otras personas, hay equipos de básquetbol, béisbol, voleibol.

Horas

lunes a viernes: 6:00 de la mañana a 9:00 de la noche.

sábado: 7:00 de la mañana a 6:00 de la tarde.

Membresías.

Hay membresías personales y familiares. Puedes pedir la lista de los precios.

Dirección: Calle Mella, 100. Santo Domingo.

Teléfono: (809) 583-1492.

REPASO: ACTIVIDAD 1 – LISTEN AND UNDERSTAND

Level 1 Textbook p. 322

TXT CD 6, Track 11

Level 1B Textbook p. 128

Level 1B TXT CD 1, Track 20

Escucha una entrevista entre Tina y Sergio Martínez, un atleta famoso. Luego escoge la respuesta correcta.

Tina: Hola, señor Martínez. Usted es jugador de fútbol americano. ¿Practica otros deportes?

Sergio: Sí, juego al básquetbol y al tenis con mis amigos.

Tina: El fútbol americano es peligroso, ¿no?

Sergio: Sí, es un poco peligroso, pero también es divertido.

Audio Scripts

Tina: ¿Conoce usted a muchos de sus aficionados?

Sergio: No, no conozco a muchos, pero son todos muy simpáticos.

Tina: ¿Le gusta hacer otras actividades?

Sergio: Sí, yo nado mucho. También sé dibujar muy bien.

Tina: ¿Ah, sí? Usted es un atleta muy interesante.

Sergio: Gracias, señorita

WORKBOOK SCRIPTS
WB CD 3

INTEGRACIÓN HABLAR

Level 1 Workbook p. 255
Level 1B Workbook p. 59
WB CD 3, Track 21

Listen to Alejandro's telephone message to Club Arco iris. Take notes.

FUENTE 2

WB CD 3, Track 22

¡Buenas tardes! Me llamo Alejandro Parra y quiero jugar al béisbol en el Club Arco iris. También practico otros deportes. No me gusta jugar al tenis, pero me gusta nadar. También patino en línea de vez en cuando. Es divertido ser atlético. ¿Y el béisbol? Yo lo juego mucho, ¡casi todos los días! Si me invitan, ¡voy a jugar!

INTEGRACIÓN ESCRIBIR

Level 1 Workbook p. 256
Level 1B Workbook p. 60
WB CD 3, Track 23

Listen to Gustavo's coach speaking about the championship match on a radio show. Take notes.

FUENTE 2

WB CD 3, Track 24

¡Hola! Gracias por invitarme.Todos pensamos mucho en el partido de hoy. Es un gran partido. Los aficionados están emocionados. Pero todos tienen que comprender que es divertido ganar pero está bien si perdemos. No podemos ganar todos los partidos, pero siempre podemos jugar bien. No podemos estar nerviosos porque sabemos que los jugadores tranquilos juegan mejor. Si jugamos como los campeones, vamos a ganar. Pero si perdemos, también vamos a estar contentos.

ESCUCHAR A, ACTIVIDAD 1

Level 1 Workbook p. 257
Level 1B Workbook p. 61
WB CD 3, Track 25

Listen to Ernesto. Place an "x" next to the things he says he needs for his favorite sport.

Hola, me llamo Ernesto y hoy es mi cumpleaños. Mis padres dicen que voy a recibir las cosas que necesito para practicar mi deporte favorito. Yo juego al béisbol. Quiero un guante nuevo y un bate muy bonito. No sé qué voy a recibir de mi hermano, todavía necesito un casco nuevo y una pelota.

ESCUCHAR A, ACTIVIDAD 2

Level 1 Workbook p. 257
Level 1B Workbook p. 61
WB CD 3, Track 26

Listen to Ángel. Then complete the sentences by filling in the correct word.

Hola, me llamo Ángel. Hoy estoy en el centro comercial. Mañana es el cumpleaños de mi hijo y él necesita unas cosas para jugar a su deporte. Tengo que encontrar un guante para su cumpleaños. A él le gustan muchos deportes pero le gusta más el béisbol.

ESCUCHAR B, ACTIVIDAD 1

Level 1 Workbook p. 258
Level 1B Workbook p. 62
WB CD 3, Track 27

Listen to Julio. Complete the table with the sport that each student plays.

Mis amigos son chicos muy atléticos. Ellos saben qué es importante practicar deportes. Ana nada todos los sábados. Miguel y Jimena juegan al béisbol. Lucas y Susana practican básquetbol. Ellos son muy altos. Andrea patina en línea y Marcos juega al fútbol americano.

ESCUCHAR B, ACTIVIDAD 2

Level 1 Workbook p. 258
Level 1B Workbook p. 62
WB CD 3, Track 28

Listen to the conversation between Ana and Jorge. Take notes. Then answer the questions below in complete sentences.

Ana: Hola, Jorge. ¿Quieres ir al estadio?

Jorge: Hola, Ana. Sí, ¿por qué?, ¿quién juega?

Ana: Juega el equipo de básquetbol de mi hermano Marcos. Ellos son los campeones todos los años. Y yo sé que este año también. ¡Vamos a ver a los ganadores!

Jorge: ¿Eres una aficionada?

Ana: Me gusta el básquetbol pero no soy aficionada. Mi hermano mira muchos partidos de básquetbol en la televisión pero yo no.

ESCUCHAR C, ACTIVIDAD 1

Level 1 Workbook p. 259
Level 1B Workbook p. 63
WB CD 3, Track 29

Listen to Lucas and take notes. Then write what day(s) he does the following activities.

Hola, me llamo Lucas y soy atleta. ¡Me gustan mucho los deportes! Estoy muy ocupado con los deportes. Los sábados juego al fútbol americano toda la tarde y los domingos practico tenis en la mañana. Practico voleibol. Los lunes juego al básquetbol con mis amigos. Los miércoles en la tarde patino en línea y los jueves después de las clases juego en el equipo de béisbol.

Audio Scripts

ESCUCHAR C, ACTIVIDAD 2

Level 1 Workbook p. 259
Level 1B Workbook p. 63
WB CD 3, Track 30

Listen to the conversation between Débora and her mother. Take notes. Then answer the following questions.

Susana: ¡Débora!, ¿dónde está tu hermano?

Débora: Mamá, hoy es lunes. Nicolás practica deportes todo el día. Los lunes no lo vemos en casa. Son las cuatro, es la hora en que patina.

Susana: Aquí están sus patines en línea. Él no sabe que están aquí. Tiene que venir a buscarlos. ¿Conoces el lugar donde patina?

Débora: Sí, está cerca de la escuela. Él llega siempre a las cuatro. Todo su equipo patina allí... no, todos no: Jorge dice que es peligroso y no va nunca. Pero otros sí.

ASSESSMENT SCRIPTS
TEST CD 2

LESSON 1 TEST: ESCUCHAR ACTIVIDAD A

Modified Assessment Book p. 206
On-level Assessment Book p. 261
Pre-AP Assessment Book p. 206
TEST CD 2, Track 7

Listen to the following audio. Then complete Activity A.

¡Buenas tardes, chicos! Soy el señor García. Hay quince jugadores en el equipo. Tenemos que ir de lunes a viernes de las tres a las cinco de la tarde. Hay que llegar temprano y necesitan venir todos los días con sus bates y guantes. Cada sábado tenemos un partido a la una en el estadio. Y el domingo, pueden descansar.

Chicos, el béisbol es un deporte para atletas. Ustedes son atletas y van a ser campeones. No vamos a ganar siempre. Si perdemos está bien. Pero vamos a jugar bien y vamos a trabajar mucho para comprender bien las reglas del juego. Somos un equipo. Tenemos que trabajar mucho.

LESSON 1 TEST: ESCUCHAR ACTIVIDAD B

Modified Assessment Book p. 206
On-level Assessment Book p. 261
Pre-AP Assessment Book p. 206
TEST CD 2, Track 8

Listen to the following audio. Then complete Activity B.

Flora: ¿Jugamos al tenis?

Javier: Yo no sé jugar al tenis.

Flora: Tú juegas muy bien al básquetbol. Vamos al gimnasio.

Javier: Me gusta mucho el básquetbol pero es domingo y siempre hay muchas personas en el gimnasio el domingo. No quiero jugar al básquetbol.

Flora: ¿Patinamos en línea en el parque?

Javier: Necesito mi casco y no sé dónde está.

Flora: Sí, necesitas un casco para patinar en línea. Bueno, Javier. Yo voy al gimnasio. ¿Qué vas a hacer?

Javier: Estoy bien aquí. Estoy un poco cansado. Voy a mirar la televisión.

HERITAGE LEARNERS SCRIPTS
HL CDS 2 & 4

INTEGRACIÓN HABLAR

Level 1 HL Workbook p. 257
Level 1B HL Workbook p. 61
HL CD 2, Track 9

Escucha el mensaje que le dejó el profesor de educación física Rolando Puentes a su esposa Magali. Toma notas mientras escuchas y luego responde a las preguntas.

FUENTE 2

HL CD 2, Track 10

Hola, Magali. El director de la escuela me acaba de autorizar cien dólares para los premios del torneo intramuros. Necesito por lo menos tres artículos para los equipos que ganen el primer, segundo y tercer lugar. Llámame al celular si tienes preguntas. Gracias.

INTEGRACIÓN ESCRIBIR

Level 1 HL Workbook p. 258
Level 1B HL Workbook p. 62
HL CD 2, Track 11

Escucha lo que dice Fernando Hernández, un joven dominicano que sueña con llegar al béisbol de las ligas mayores. Toma apuntes y después completa la actividad.

FUENTE 2

HL CD 2, Track 12

Éste es mi segundo año en la academia de béisbol y mi sueño es poder viajar a los Estados Unidos el próximo año a jugar en las ligas americanas. Algunas personas me dicen que estoy muy joven, pero yo creo que soy listo. Mis jugadores favoritos son los Medias Rojas de Boston, aunque mi pelotero preferido es David Ortiz. Veo todos los juegos que pasan por televisión. Son mis grandes campeones. Para mi cumpleaños mi padre me regaló un bate firmado por los campeones del 2004.

LESSON 1 TEST: ESCUCHAR ACTIVIDAD A

HL Assessment Book p. 212
HL CD 4, Track 7

Escucha el siguiente audio. Luego, completa la Actividad A.

Rita: Hola, Alberto. ¿Qué haces por aquí?

Alberto: Quiero comprarle un regalo a mi primo, Enrique. Es un gran atleta. Le gustan todos los deportes y juega a casi todos.

Rita: ¿Juega al béisbol?

Alberto: Sí.

Rita: ¿Por qué no le compras un bate, o un guante...?

Alberto: No, no. Tiene muchos bates y guantes.

Rita: ¿Le gusta patinar?

Alberto: Sí, mucho.

Rita: ¿Por qué no le compras unos patines en línea? Estos son muy buenos.

Audio Scripts

Alberto: Pero cuestan mucho. No tengo tanto dinero.

Rita: ¿Juega al fútbol americano?

Alberto: Sí.

Rita: ¿Necesita un casco? ¿O tal vez esta pelota con los autógrafos del equipo campeón?

Alberto: Tiene muchos cascos y a Enrique no le gusta ese equipo.

Rita: ¿También juega al fútbol?

Alberto: Claro.

Rita: ¿Por qué no le compras un libro sobre la historia de fútbol? Mira. Este libro es muy interesante, ¿no?

Alberto: Sí. Aquí hablan de los equipos y jugadores famosos, hay información sobre los estadios y muchas fotos de todas las Copas Mundiales. Buena idea, Rita, gracias.

Rita: ¡De nada!

LESSON 1 TEST: ESCUCHAR ACTIVIDAD B

HL Assessment Book p. 212

HL CD 4, Track 8

No sé qué hacer. Quiero jugar al tenis, pero no tengo una buena raqueta y no sé dónde están las pelotas de tenis. También me gusta el béisbol pero no sé dónde están el bate y el guante. Si juego al fútbol necesito un buen casco porque sin el casco es peligroso jugar al fútbol americano. Y no tengo casco. Mis amigos quieren patinar, pero no tengo patines en línea y los nuevos cuestan muchísimo. Y si juego al básquetbol tengo que llamar a varios amigos para ver si quieren jugar. Y no me gusta jugar al voleibol. No sé qué hacer... ¡Ay! Me gusta nadar. Puedo practicar la natación sin problemas. La piscina está cerca de casa y no necesito bates, raquetas, cascos o patines. Sólo necesito el traje de baño. ¿Dónde está?

Audio Scripts

PRESENTACIÓN DE VOCABULARIO

Level 1 Textbook pp. 326-327

Level 1B Textbook pp. 132-134

TXT CD 6, Track 12

A. Soy Isabel. En la playa Mario y yo siempre usamos bloqueador de sol. Si no lo usamos, tomar el sol puede ser malo para la piel.

B. En la República Dominicana hay muchas actividades que son buenas para la salud. Yo camino, pero también puedes hacer esquí acuático o bucear. A Mario le gusta levantar pesas.

C. Si hacemos actividades en la playa, usamos bloqueador de sol en todo el cuerpo: la nariz, las orejas, los brazos, las piernas...

D. Mario es fuerte pero ahora está herido. Le duele mucho el tobillo.

E. Yo soy muy sana pero de vez en cuando estoy enferma.

¡A RESPONDER!

Level 1 Textbook p. 327

TXT CD 6, Track 13

Level 1B Textbook p. 134

Level 1B TXT CD, Track 21

Levántate. Escucha al atleta profesional hablar de lo que le duele. Señala las partes del cuerpo que menciona.

1. Me duele el brazo.

2. Me duele el tobillo.

3. Me duele la mano.

4. Me duele la rodilla.

5. Me duele la pierna.

6. Me duele la nariz.

7. Me duele el pie.

TELEHISTORIA ESCENA 1

Level 1 Textbook p. 329

Level 1B Textbook p. 136

TXT CD 6, Track 14

Mario: ¡Tenemos que ser los primeros aficionados en el estadio!

Isabel: Mario, ¿sabes montar en bicicleta?

Mario: Sí, sí, ¡es fácil!

Isabel: ¡Necesitas el casco!

Mario: ¡No estoy herido!

Isabel: Pero, ¿y el tobillo? ¿Y la pierna?

Mario: Soy fuerte y sano...

Isabel: Y la cabeza, ¿Mario? ¡Tienes la piel muy roja! ¡La nariz! Abre la boca. ¿Puedes caminar?

Mario: Sí. Me duele un poco el pie... pero puedo caminar.

Isabel: No, no debes caminar.

Mario: Pero... ¡Y Trini Salgado!

Isabel: ¿Trini Salgado? ¡Un autógrafo no es importante! Vamos...

TELEHISTORIA ESCENA 2

Level 1 Textbook p. 334

Level 1B Textbook p. 142

TXT CD 6, Track 15

Doctora: ¿Mario Álvarez? ¿Está usted enfermo?

Isabel: Le duelen la pierna y la cabeza. Lo ayudé a caminar.

Doctora: ¿Qué hiciste?

Isabel: Pues, montó en su bicicleta... ¡cerca de unas frutas!

Mario: Monté en mi bicicleta...

Doctora: ¿Llevaste un casco?

Isabel: Sí, ¡pero Mario piensa que es Lance Armstrong!

Mario: Isabel, ¡el señor de las frutas caminó delante de mi bicicleta!

Isabel: Y allí... ¡Pum!

Doctora: Mario, ¿sabes montar en bicicleta?

Mario: Sí, es fácil.

Doctora: ¿Te gustó?

Mario: Ahora estoy herido, ¡pero me gustó!

Doctora: Para la salud de tu amigo, no más bicicletas, ¡por favor!

ACTIVIDAD 13 (16) - MUCHAS PREGUNTAS

Level 1 Textbook p. 337

TXT CD 6, Track 16

Level 1B Textbook p. 146

Level 1B TXT CD, Track 22

Mario quiere saber lo que hiciste ayer. Escucha sus preguntas y escribe tus respuestas.

Modelo

Mario: ¿Pagaste el almuerzo?

Chica 1: Si, pagué el almuerzo.

No, no pagué el almuerzo.

1. ¿A qué hora llegaste a la escuela ayer?

2. ¿Sacaste buenas o malas notas?

3. ¿A qué hora almorzaste?

4. ¿Comenzaste la tarea?

5. ¿Buscaste ropa nueva?

6. ¿A qué jugaste?

PRONUNCIACIÓN

Level 1 Textbook p. 337

Level 1B Textbook p. 146

TXT CD 6, Track 17

La letra **g** con **e**, **i**

Before **e** and **i**, the **g** in Spanish is pronounced like the Spanish **j**.

Listen and repeat.

ge

inteligente

Argentina

Jorge

general

gi

gimnasio

digital

página

Sergio

Jorge corre en el gimnasio.

Regina tiene una cámara digital.

TELEHISTORIA COMPLETA

Level 1 Textbook p. 339

Level 1B Textbook p. 148

TXT CD 6, Track 18

Escena 1 - Resumen

Mario está herido y no puede ir con Isabel al estadio para ver a Trini Salgado.

Escena 2 - Resumen

Isabel ayuda a Mario a caminar. A él le duelen la pierna y la cabeza. Ellos hablan con una doctora.

Escena 3

Doctora: El tobillo está bien. ¿Te duele la rodilla?

Mario: No. Un poco.

Audio Scripts

Doctora: No puedes jugar al fútbol, y no puedes jugar al béisbol por cuatro semanas.

Mario: ¿Puedo levantar pesas?

Doctora: Levantar pesas, sí, con los brazos. Con las piernas, no…

Isabel: Muchas gracias, doctora. Adiós.

Mario: ¡Ay, el autógrafo para Alicia! Comencé a...

Isabel: Sí, Mario, lo siento. Comenzaste a buscar a Trini, pero ¿qué podemos hacer?

Isabel: ¿Vamos a la playa mañana? El mar es bueno para los enfermos.

Mario: ¡No estoy enfermo!

ACTIVIDAD 19 (23) – INTEGRACIÓN

Level 1 Textbook p. 341

TXT CD 6, Track 19

Level 1B Textbook p. 150

Level 1B TXT CD, Track 23

Lee el artículo y escucha la entrevista. Compara lo que tú hiciste durante la semana para la salud con lo que estas personas hicieron. Decide si eres tan sano o sana como ellos.

FUENTE 2

TXT CD 6, Track 20

Level 1B TXT CD, Track 24

Listen and take notes

¿Qué deportes practicó la chica?

¿Qué almorzó?

¿Qué hiciste durante la semana para la salud?

Durante la semana practiqué muchos deportes. El lunes y el miércoles jugué al tenis con mi hermana. También caminé a la escuela. Normalmente tomo el autobús pero el lunes empecé a caminar. El sábado jugué al fútbol. Comer comida sana es difícil. ¡Me gusta mucho comer! Hoy almorcé pizza con jamón y de postre, helado de chocolate.

LECTURA CULTURAL: DOS ATLETAS DE ALTA VELOCIDAD

Level 1 Textbook pp. 342-343

Level 1B Textbook pp. 152-153

TXT CD 6, Track 21

Latinoamérica tiene una gran historia de deportes y de atletas ganadores.

Algunos practican su deporte día y noche, en las calles y pistas que están muy lejos de los aficionados y de las cámaras de televisión.

Félix Sánchez es uno de los atletas más dominantes en los 400 metros de vallas. Estadounidense de nacimiento, Sánchez decidió representar a la República Dominicana, el país de sus padres, en competiciones internacionales. En los Juegos Olímpicos del 2000 en Sydney, Australia, Félix Sánchez llegó en cuarto lugar. Para tener motivación, Sánchez prometió llevar el brazalete que llevó en Sydney hasta ganar una medalla de oro. Lo llevó por cuatro años. En los Juegos Olímpicos del 2004, ganó la primera medalla de oro para la República Dominicana y se hizo héroe nacional. Después de ganar, el triunfante Sánchez caminó delante de los aficionados con la bandera dominicana en las manos.

Muchas personas montan en bicicleta pero pocas van tan rápido como la ciclista venezolana Daniela Larreal. Ella ganó tres medallas de oro en los Juegos Bolivarianos en el 2001. En el 2003, se hizo campeona de la Copa Mundial de Ciclismo de Pista. En agosto del 2005, ella ganó otra medalla de oro en los Juegos Bolivarianos. Llegó a los 500 metros con un tiempo de 35,56 segundos. «¡Qué rico es volver a estar en unos Bolivarianos y ganar nuevamente otra medalla», comentó la campeona.

REPASO: ACTIVIDAD 1 – LISTEN AND UNDERSTAND

Level 1 Textbook p. 346

TXT CD 6, Track 22

Level 1B Textbook p. 156

Level 1B TXT CD, Track 25

Elisa describe un día en la playa. Escucha y escribe si ella hizo o no las siguientes actividades.

Ayer pasé un rato con mi familia en la playa. Mi hermana y yo usamos mucho bloqueador porque tomamos el sol. Nuestro hermano buceó en el mar. Nuestros padres caminaron, y yo almorcé con mis hermanos. Otras personas jugaron al voleibol. Yo jugué un poco con ellos. Después yo descansé. En la noche unos chicos tocaron la guitarra y nosotros cantamos con ellos. Pasamos un día muy divertido en la playa.

Modelo: usar bloqueador de sol
Elisa usó bloqueador de sol.

COMPARACIÓN CULTURAL: DEPORTES FAVORITOS

Level 1 Textbook pp. 348-349

Level 1B Textbook pp. 158-159

TXT CD 6, Track 23

República Dominicana: Felipe

Felipe: ¡Hola! Me llamo Felipe y vivo en Punta Cana, cerca del mar. Ayer pasé el día en la playa con mis amigos. Después de nadar un rato, jugamos un partido de voleibol con ocho jugadores. Mi equipo comprende las reglas pero ayer no ganó el partido. El voleibol es mi deporte favorito porque puedo jugar con mis amigos y no es peligroso.

Honduras: Gloria

Gloria: ¿Qué tal? Me llamo Gloria y vivo en La Ceiba, el lugar perfecto para practicar deportes acuáticos. Mi deporte favorito es el rafting. Uno de los mejores ríos para practicar rafting en Honduras es el río Cangreja. La semana pasada, mis hermanos y yo alquilamos una balsa para navegar el río. Es una actividad muy divertida.

Narradora: Venezuela. Agustín.

Agustín: ¡Hola! Me llamo Agustín. Soy aficionado de los deportes. Me gusta mucho el béisbol, pero me gusta más el básquetbol porque soy alto y tengo las piernas y los brazos largos. También me gusta correr y saltar. Mis amigos y yo jugamos casi todos los días en una cancha cerca de mi casa en Caracas.

REPASO: ACTIVIDAD 1 – LISTEN, UNDERSTAND AND COMPARE

Level 1 Textbook p. 350

Level 1B Textbook p. 160

TXT CD 6, Track 24

Listen to a sports broadcast from the Dominican Republic. Then answer the following questions.

Carlos: Hace sol y un poco calor aquí en el campo de béisbol. Yo soy Carlos Pérez y estoy aquí con Luis Alomar.

Luis: Gracias, Carlos. Allí en el campo está Mariano Sandoval y

Audio Scripts

tengo que decir que no hay mejor atleta en todos los equipos de Latinoamérica.

Carlos: Tienes razón, Luis. Sandoval es de San Pedro de Macorís y allí saben jugar. Él juega tan bien con el bate como juega con el guante.

Luis: ¡Sí, señor! Ayer él me explicó por qué es un jugador tan bueno. Vamos a escuchar lo que dice Mariano.

Mariano Sandoval: Sabes, no siempre tenemos guantes nuevos o cascos pero tenemos mucho corazón. No pienso que soy más fuerte que los otros jugadores o que corro más que ellos. Pero sé que trabajo más que ellos.

Carlos: Sí, Luis... Mariano es un ganador de primera clase.

WORKBOOK SCRIPTS
WB CD 3

INTEGRACIÓN HABLAR

Level 1 Workbook p. 278

Level 1B Workbook p. 82

WB CD 3, Track 31

Listen to Rodrigo's voicemail for Miriam. Take notes.

FUENTE 2

WB CD 3, Track 32

¡Hola Miriam! Soy Rodrigo. Yo estoy enfermo pero no sé qué tengo. Sé que tu padre es el doctor Salinas. ¿Puedes preguntar a tu padre por qué tengo problemas de salud? Mira, cuando corro me duelen las piernas. Y cuando juego al tenis me duelen los brazos y las rodillas. Yo siempre estoy sano, pero ahora cuando practico deportes me duele todo, de los pies a la cabeza. ¿Qué hago? Tu padre sabe qué hacer. Él sabe mucho.

INTEGRACIÓN ESCRIBIR

Level 1 Workbook p. 279

Level 1B Workbook p. 83

WB CD 3, Track 33

Listen to Beatriz's voice message to Gabriela. Take notes

FUENTE 2

WB CD 3, Track 34

¡Hola, Gabriela! Acabo de leer tu correo electrónico. Sí, es muy

divertido estar en la playa, pero tomar el sol sin bloqueador de sol es muy peligroso. Ayer yo también pasé todo el día en la playa con amigos. Pero tomé el sol con bloqueador de sol y me siento muy bien. No me duele todo el cuerpo. Tengo la piel un poco roja, pero no estoy como un tomate y no me duele la cabeza. ¿Nos vemos mañana?

ESCUCHAR A, ACTIVIDAD 1

Level 1 Workbook p. 280

Level 1B Workbook p. 84

WB CD 3, Track 35

Listen to Graciela. Then, read each sentence and answer **cierto** (true) or **falso** (false).

Ayer, mis amigos y yo pasamos todo el día en la playa. Miriam tomó el sol toda la mañana y toda la tarde. Usó muy poco bloqueador de sol y hoy está enferma. Le duelen la cabeza y la piel. Yo caminé por la playa con Ignacio pero nosotros sí usamos bloqueador de sol y unos sombreros muy grandes.

ESCUCHAR A, ACTIVIDAD 2

Level 1 Workbook p. 280

Level 1B Workbook p. 84

WB CD 3, Track 36

Listen to Miriam. Then, complete the sentences with the correct word.

Ayer tomé mucho sol. Pasé el día en la playa con una amiga y otros chicos. No pensé que el sol es tan fuerte en la playa. Cuando llegué a mi casa en la noche, mi amiga me llamó para saber de mi salud. Yo anoche le contesté "estoy bien" pero hoy estoy en cama porque me duele todo.

ESCUCHAR B, ACTIVIDAD 1

Level 1 Workbook p. 281

Level 1B Workbook p. 85

WB CD 3, Track 37

Listen to Lourdes and take notes. Then, match the people with what they did at the beach. People may have done more than one thing.

¡Que divertido el día de playa con mis amigos! Ayer celebramos mi cumpleaños en la playa. Las chicas prepararon un pastel muy grande y los chicos compraron los refrescos. Juan practicó esquí acuático y

Norma caminó por la playa. Marcos tocó su guitarra y todos nosotros cantamos en la noche. Julia y Diego bailaron. Llegué a casa muy tarde pero muy contenta.

ESCUCHAR B, ACTIVIDAD 2

Level 1 Workbook p. 281

Level 1B Workbook p. 85

WB CD 3, Track 38

Listen to Marcos. Take notes. Then, complete the sentences below.

Ayer celebramos el cumpleaños de mi mejor amiga, Lourdes. Mis amigos y yo pensamos ir a la playa. Pasamos un rato divertido. Yo toqué mi guitarra y toqué mucha música rock. Hoy me duelen las manos porque toqué mucho. Todos cantaron y terminaron el día muy cansados pero felices.

ESCUCHAR C, ACTIVIDAD 1

Level 1 Workbook p. 282

Level 1B Workbook p. 86

WB CD 3, Track 39

Listen to the doctor and take notes. Then, complete the table with the causes of each person's pain.

Hoy llegaron muchos chicos a verme. A todos les duele algo. A unos chicos les duele el estómago porque cenaron comida poco nutritiva. A otros chicos les duele la piel porque tomaron el sol sin bloqueador del sol. A otros les duele la cabeza o los ojos porque estudiaron toda la noche. A otros chicos les duelen los brazos porque levantaron pesas. A otros les duelen las orejas porque escucharon música fuerte.

ESCUCHAR C, ACTIVIDAD 2

Level 1 Workbook p. 282

Level 1B Workbook p. 86

WB CD 3, Track 40

Listen to Luis' conversation with the doctor. Take notes. Then, answer the following questions.

Doctor: Hola, Luis ¿Qué te duele?

Luis: Hola, doctor. Me duele mucho el estómago.

Doctor: Vamos a ver qué pasa. ¿Qué almorzaste ayer?

Luis: Almorcé una pizza muy grande con refresco. Después leche con

Audio Scripts

cereal y pastel del cumpleaños de mi hermana.

Doctor: ¿Cuándo celebraron el cumpleaños de tu hermana?

Luis: La semana pasada. Encontré el pastel en la cocina y bueno, usted sabe.

Doctor: Tienes que pensar más en tu salud.

ASSESSMENT SCRIPTS
TEST CD 2

LESSON 2 TEST: ESCUCHAR
ACTIVIDAD A

Modified Assessment Book p. 218

On-level Assessment Book p. 278

Pre-AP Assessment Book p. 218

TEST CD 2, Track 9

Listen to the following audio. Then complete Activity A.

1. ¿Cómo estás Guadalupe? ¿Estás bien?

   No, maestro. Levanté pesas ayer y ahora me duelen los brazos.

2. ¿Y tú, Felipe? ¿Estás herido?

   Yo jugué al fútbol ayer y me duele mucho el tobillo.

3. ¿Qué tal Marisa?

   Toqué la guitarra todo el día y ahora me duelen las manos.

4. ¿Cómo estás, Vicente?

   Estudié mucho anoche. Me duele la cabeza.

5. ¿Juana, tú estudiaste también?

   No, maestro. Pero estoy enferma. Descansé mucho anoche pero me duele el estómago. Hoy no puedo comer.

LESSON 2 TEST: ESCUCHAR
ACTIVIDAD B

Modified Assessment Book p. 218

On-level Assessment Book p. 278

Pre-AP Assessment Book p. 218

TEST CD 2, Track 10

Listen to the following audio. Then complete Activity B.

Pasamos todo el día en la playa. Mis amigos nadaron y bucearon en el mar. Yo no sé nadar muy bien, entonces descansé en la playa y tomé el sol. Mis amigos descansaron y

tomaron el sol también. Después jugamos al voleibol en la playa. Me gusta mucho el voleibol. Es mi deporte favorito.

UNIT 6 TEST: ESCUCHAR
ACTIVIDAD A

Modified Assessment Book p. 230

On-level Assessment Book p. 290

Pre-AP Assessment Book p. 230

TEST CD 2, Track 11

Listen to the following audio. Then complete Activity A.

Verónica: Durante el verano hay muchas clases en el gimnasio. ¿Qué tal si tomamos clases de natación?

Marta: Ya sé nadar muy bien. No necesito clases.

Verónica: También hay clases de tenis. El gimnasio tiene muchas canchas.

Marta: Pero, Verónica, no tengo raqueta.

Verónica: Bueno, ¿te gusta patinar en línea? Hay clases todos los domingos.

Marta: Ay, no me gusta, y es un deporte muy peligroso.

Verónica: Pero, puedes llevar un casco.

Marta: Verónica, no sé patinar en línea y me duelen las rodillas.

Verónica: Marta, al voleibol juegas, ¿verdad? Hay un equipo de chicas que juega todos los sábados a las tres.

Marta: Sí, conozco a las chicas del equipo. El voleibol es muy divertido y tengo todo lo que necesito para jugar al voleibol.

Verónica: ¿Qué necesitas, Marta?

Marta: Pues, tengo las dos manos.

UNIT 6 TEST: ESCUCHAR
ACTIVIDAD B

Modified Assessment Book p. 230

On-level Assessment Book p. 290

Pre-AP Assessment Book p. 230

TEST CD 2, Track 12

Listen to the following audio. Then complete Activity B.

Hola, me llamo Cristina. Soy de Nueva York, pero mis abuelos son de la República Dominicana. Ayer llegué a la casa de mis abuelos.

Anoche mi abuela no cocinó. Mis abuelos y yo encontramos un restaurante muy bueno cerca del mar. Hoy en la mañana mis primos y yo nadamos en la playa. Mi abuela tomó mucho sol pero usó bloqueador de sol. Mi abuelo jugó al voleibol en la playa. Mañana, mis abuelos, mis primos y yo vamos a ver un partido de béisbol en el estadio.

HERITAGE LEARNERS SCRIPTS
HL CDS 2 & 4

INTEGRACIÓN HABLAR

Level 1 HL Workbook p. 280

Level 1B HL Workbook p. 84

HL CD 2, Track 13

Escucha el mensaje que dejó Alberto, un programador de computadoras, a su entrenadora Mireya. Puedes tomar notas mientras escuchas y después prepárate para completar la actividad.

FUENTE 2

HL CD 2, Track 14

Hola, Mireya, te llamo para avisarte que no voy a poder asistir a la sesión de hoy. Me duele la espalda y tengo el cuello inmóvil. No sé si no dormí bien o si es porque trabajo tanto en esta computadora. Tengo el cuerpo hecho una tabla, desde la cabeza a los pies. Todo me molesta. Espero poder levantar pesas mañana. Hoy trataré de caminar un poco, en cuanto termine este proyecto. Hasta mañana.

INTEGRACIÓN ESCRIBIR

Level 1 HL Workbook p. 281

Level 1B HL Workbook p. 85

HL CD 2, Track 15

Escucha una parte del programa de radio «Salud para vivir» de la doctora Betina Cortés. Toma notas mientras escuchas y luego responde a las preguntas

FUENTE 2

HL CD 2, Track 16

Gracias a todos por escuchar este programa. Les habla la doctora Betina Cortés y antes de los anuncios respondía a la pregunta de Sara... Sí, como decía, cada deporte tiene sus beneficios particulares, pero la natación es uno de los deportes

Copyright © by McDougal Littell, a division of Houghton Mifflin Company.

Audio Scripts

más nobles porque no martiriza tus coyunturas como otros, por ejemplo, correr. Pero si a ti lo que te gusta es correr, asegúrate de llevar zapatos cómodos y hechos para este deporte. Es importantísimo preocuparse por el calzado porque no cualquier zapato tenis está hecho para aguantar el trote, el impacto en la planta de los pies y en las rodillas. Además, si quieres perder peso, trata de levantar pesas, llevar una dieta sana y nada de abusos. Y claro, mantente bajo supervisión médica…

LESSON 1 TEST: ESCUCHAR ACTIVIDAD A

HL Assessment Book p. 224

HL CD 4, Track 9

Escucha el siguiente audio. Luego, completa la actividad A.

Gloria: ¿Qué hiciste ayer, Raúl?

Raúl: Lo pasé muy bien, Gloria. Comencé el día con un desayuno muy sano: mucha fruta y un jugo de naranja. Luego caminé por la playa.

Gloria: ¿Cuánto tiempo caminaste?

Raúl: Empecé a las ocho y terminé a las once.

Gloria: ¡Tres horas! ¿Y luego?

Raúl: Para tener los brazos más fuertes, levanté pesas en casa durante una hora.

Gloria: Y después, ¿almorzaste?

Raúl: No, después buceé con mi hermana. Buceamos por más de dos horas. Después almorzamos en la playa.

Gloria: ¡Qué bien! ¿Y luego?

Raúl: Jugué al fútbol con mis primos por la tarde.

Gloria: ¿Descansaste después?

Raúl: No. Hice esquí acuático hasta las siete. ¡Ahh! Y anoche también jugué al básquetbol.

Gloria: ¿Y qué tal?

Raúl: Bien, pero hoy me duelen las piernas y los brazos.

Gloria: Claro, practicaste muchos deportes ayer.

Raúl: Y también me duele la piel un poco porque no usé bloqueador de sol.

ACTIVIDAD B

HL Assessment Book p. 224

HL CD 4, Track 10

Escucha el siguiente audio. Luego, completa la actividad B.

Felipe: Hola, Juan Carlos, ¿quieres bucear conmigo esta tarde?

Juan Carlos: No, lo siento, no puedo. No sé bucear.

Felipe: ¿Qué tal si hacemos esquí acuático? ¿Te interesa?

Juan Carlos: No, no puedo. No sé nadar.

Felipe: ¿Por qué no caminamos por la playa?

Juan Carlos: No, lo siento, pero no puedo. Me duelen las rodillas.

Felipe: ¿Quieres jugar al voleibol en la playa?

Juan Carlos: No, gracias. También me duelen las piernas.

Felipe: ¿Y si levantamos pesas?

Juan Carlos: ¡Imposible! Me duelen mucho los brazos.

Felipe: Bueno… ¿y si tomamos el sol? Hace un día estupendo.

Juan Carlos: No, lo siento. No traigo el bloqueador de sol. Me voy a casa.

Felipe: ¿Vas a almorzar?

Juan Carlos: No, Felipe. Me duele el estómago. Voy a descansar.

UNIT 6 TEST: ESCUCHAR ACTIVIDAD A

HL Assessment Book p. 236

HL CD 4, Track 11

Escucha el siguiente audio. Luego, completa la actividad A.

Raúl: Felipe, ¿sabes quién ganó el partido de béisbol ayer?

Felipe: Lo siento, Raúl, pero no tengo idea. Ayer jugué al tenis con Claudia toda la mañana.

Raúl: ¿Sabes qué equipo ganó el partido de básquetbol el viernes?

Felipe: Sí, porque vi el partido en la televisión. Ganaron Los Osos de Santo Domingo. Noventa y nueve a noventa y ocho.

Raúl: ¿Y el partido de tenis el sábado? ¿Entre Ortega y Ramírez? Conoces a estos atletas, ¿verdad?

Felipe: Sí, los conozco, pero no sé cuál de los dos ganó porque comenzaron a jugar a las diez de la mañana y a las nueve siempre salgo a nadar durante dos horas.

Raúl: Sí, sí, ya lo sé… pero sabes algo del partido de fútbol americano,

¿no? Los mejores equipos jugaron anoche.

Felipe: Pues, no… porque anoche jugué al voleibol de cinco a ocho. ¿Sabes que ahora somos los campeones de la ciudad?

Raúl: ¡Qué bien! Pero quiero saber quiénes ganaron los partidos. ¿Sabes algo del partido de fútbol entre la República Dominicana y México? Jugaron el viernes a la misma hora que el partido de básquetbol.

Felipe: Lo siento, Raúl, no sé quién ganó. Pero mira, ¿por qué no preguntas a Enrique? ¿Lo conoces?

Raúl: ¡Claro! Enrique es el atleta número uno de la escuela.

Felipe: Sí, y sabe todo sobre los deportes, los atletas, los partidos y los campeonatos. Ahora viene.

Raúl: Oye, Enrique, ¿sabes quién ganó el partido de béisbol…

ACTIVIDAD B

HL Assessment Book p. 236

HL CD 4, Track 12

Escucha el siguiente audio. Luego, completa la actividad B.

¡Ay! Me duele todo el cuerpo. ¿Por qué? ¡Porque el fin de semana practiqué todos los deportes del mundo! Empecé el viernes, después de las clases. Patiné dos horas con Ana María y Teresa y luego jugué al fútbol con mis hermanitos. El sábado pasé el día en la playa. Primero, buceé casi toda la mañana con una prima. Luego almorzamos al lado del mar. Después de almorzar practiqué el esquí acuático, que es muy divertido. Después de hacer esquí acuático, nadé en nuestra piscina. Por la tarde también jugué al básquetbol. Por la noche, Blanca y yo patinamos en línea porque ella es la campeona de patinaje de nuestra escuela. Patinamos hasta muy tarde. El domingo monté en bicicleta casi toda la mañana y luego jugué al tenis con mi tía que juega muy bien. Nadé un poco y después caminé por la playa, donde luego todos jugamos al voleibol. Antes de dormir, levanté pesas. Pero ahora me duelen los brazos, las manos, las piernas y las rodillas… ¡No pienso practicar más deportes hasta… por lo menos mañana!

Map/Culture Activities   *República Dominicana*

1 The Dominican Republic occupies two-thirds of Hispaniola. Which bodies of water surround the island? Locate them and write their names on the map.

HAITÍ

REPÚBLICA DOMINICANA

2 The Dominican Republic's capital is located on the island's southern coast. Locate this city and write its name on the map.

3 Punta Cana, an ocean resort, and Juan Dolio, also on the coast, are two other cities in the Dominican Republic. Locate them and write their names on the map.

4 What other Spanish-speaking islands can be found near the Dominican Republic?

_____

_____

_____

_____

_____

Map/Culture Activities *República Dominicana*

5 Use the information from your textbook to choose the answer below that best completes each sentence.

1. En Santo Domingo, el Altar de la Patria representa la independencia de la República Dominicana de _____ .
   a. Cuba   **b.** Haití   **c.** Estados Unidos

2. La República Dominicana comparte (*shares*) la isla Hispaniola con _____ .
   a. Haití   **b.** Puerto Rico   **c.** Cuba

3. Oscar de la Renta es famoso por su _____ .
   a. música   **b.** ropa   **c.** arte

4. Juan Luis Guerra es famoso por su _____ .
   a. música   **b.** arte   **c.** comida

6 Many people consider baseball to be the national pastime of the United States. On page 300, your book mentions that baseball is also considered the Dominican Republic's national sport. Why do you think that is? How is the baseball season in the Dominican Republic different from the one in the United States? Why?

_____
_____
_____
_____
_____

UNIDAD 6

Map/Culture Activities

Map/Culture Activities Answer Key

REPÚBLICA DOMINICANA

Page 83

OCÉANO ATLÁNTICO

HAITÍ

Santo Domingo

Punta Cana

Juan Dolio

REPÚBLICA DOMINICANA

MAR CARIBE

❶ Refer to map above.

❷ Refer to map above.

❸ Refer to map above.

❹ Cuba and Puerto Rico

Page 84

❺

   1. b

   2. a

   3. b

   4. a

❻ Answers will vary, but students should be able to infer that the two countries share baseball as a national sport because of their proximity. They also should be able to state that their baseball season begins just as ours is ending because the weather in the Dominican Republic is different than in most of the United States.

Fine Art Activities

Muchacho con cachucha, Jaime Colson

Jaime Colson was born in the Dominican Republic in 1901. He traveled and worked extensively in Spain, France, Mexico, Cuba, and Venezuela before returning to settle permanently in his homeland. Throughout his career he experimented with various artistic styles, including cubism and surrealism. Many of his works show the influence of Hispañola's predominant Creole culture. *Muchacho con cachucha* reflects Colson's fundamental interest in painting people.

Examine *Muchacho con cachucha* and complete the following activities.

1. This painting is composed almost entirely of a young man's face. Who do you think this person is? How old might he be? What are his interests? Write a detailed description of the subject's background.

   _____

   _____

   _____

   _____

2. The boy in Colson's painting appears to be focused intently on something. Observe the upward tilt of his head and the look in his eyes. Describe who or what you think he is looking at and explain why you think this.

   _____

   _____

   _____

   _____

Muchacho con cachucha (1958), Jaime Colson. Tinta sobre papel, 32 cm x 25 cm. Colección Museo Bellapart, Santo Domingo, República Dominicana.

Fine Art Activities

Una madre, Cándido Bidó

Dominican artist Cándido Bidó uses art to celebrate the commonalities between the African, Hispanic, and native Arawak cultures that make up his country's population. He often depicts his subjects in natural environments and believes that art should be accessible to all people. *Una madre* shows Bidó's characteristically simple style of painting and contains the bright colors that he creates and mixes himself.

Complete the following activities based on your analysis of *Una madre*.

1. Discuss the use of color in *Una madre*.
    a. Identify the dominant colors in the painting. What mood do you think Bidó hoped to achieve by using these colors?

    _____

    _____

    b. Bidó uses a limited color palette, but achieves a range of effects. Explain the different ways in which the artist repeats the color blue.

    _____

    _____

2. The sun is often featured in Bidó's paintings. What is the role of the sun in this painting? How does it fulfill this role? Use specific examples from the painting to explain your answer.

    _____

    _____

    _____

    _____

Una madre, Cándido Bidó. Acrylic, 40″ x 50″. Courtesy of Cándido Bidó Galería De Arte.

Fine Art Activities

Sin título, Clara Ledesma

Clara Ledesma was born in the Dominican Republic in 1924. She is one of a few Dominican women to have gained international artistic notoriety. Many of her later works, like *Sin título*, explore the African heritage of the island and include the colors and images of a dream or fantasy. She often is credited with creating an alternate, mythical world in her art by inviting the viewer to imagine a story behind her paintings.

1. Ledesma is known for her use of vibrant colors. Study the colors in *Sin título* and the way in which a single color may appear in a number of different forms. Use specific examples to tell how the artist uses white, red, blue, and yellow to achieve visual balance in the painting.

    _____

    _____

    _____

    _____

    _____

2. Look at the landscape and the way in which the three women occupy the space around them. How has the artist created a unique world in *Sin título*? Describe the features of the painting that make it seem otherworldly and explain how this is accomplished.

    _____

    _____

    _____

    _____

Sin título (1960), Clara Ledesma. Oleo sobre línea, 135 cm x 198 cm. Colección Museo Bellapart, Santo Domingo, República Dominicana.

Fine Art Activities

Paisaje de lluvia, Darío Suro

Considered to be one of the fathers of Dominican painting, Darío Suro worked as an artist and art critic for much of his life. Born in 1917, Suro began his artistic training under his uncle, and lived and studied in Europe and Mexico before settling in the United States. His art often explores the various geographic, social, and human elements that make up the Caribbean region.

Study the painting *Paisaje de lluvia*, by Darío Suro, and complete the following activities.

1. Answer the following questions about the artist's technique in *Paisaje de lluvia*.
   a. How does Suro create an illusion of depth in the painting?

   _____

   _____

   b. *Paisaje de lluvia* does not illustrate rain in a conventional way. Describe the techniques Suro has employed to suggest a heavy downpour.

   _____

   _____

2. What characteristic feature of your own landscape would you choose to paint? Explain the colors and techniques you would use to illustrate your surroundings.

   _____

   _____

   _____

   _____

Paisaje de lluvia (1940), Darío Suro. Oleo/tela, 20″ x 28.5″. Courtesy of Colección Museo Bellapart, Santo Domingo, República Dominicana.

Fine Art Activities Answer Key

MUCHACHO CON CACHUCHA, JAIME COLSON, page 86

1. Answers will vary.

2. Answers will vary. Students should be able to explain their answers.

UNA MADRE, CÁNDIDO BIDÓ, page 87

1a. The dominant color is blue, which students may describe as serene or calm.

b. Answers will vary. The color blue is altered by the addition of dots and lines, by the addition of light or dark pigment, etc.

2. Answers will vary. The sun is both symbolic and functional. It may symbolize growth and warmth, and helps distinguish different shades of blue by creating a pretext of light and shadow.

SIN TÍTULO, CLARA LEDESMA, page 88

1. Answers will vary. The colors yellow, white, and red help divide the painting into thirds. Left to right they appear in 1) a plant or tree, 2) a woman's dress and 3) a boat. The color blue is scattered in plants, water, boats, and sky throughout the painting.

2. Answers will vary. The plants and birds are wild and dream-like, some of the women appear to be floating, etc.

PAISAJE DE LLUVIA, DARÍO SURO, page 89

1a. Answers may vary. The subtle use of light and dark helps create depth.

b. The paint is applied thickly and at an angle, suggesting rain. The painting as a whole appears foggy, as if seen through a wash of rain.

2. Answers will vary.

UNIDAD 6

Fine Art Activities Answer Key

Copyright © by McDougal Littell, a division of Houghton Mifflin Company.

Unidad 6
Fine Art Activities Answer Key

90

¡Avancemos! 1
Unit Resource Book

Date: _____

Dear Family:

We are about to begin *Unidad 6* of the Level 1 *¡Avancemos!*
program. It focuses on authentic culture and real-life communication
using Spanish in the Dominican Republic. It practices reading, writing,
listening, and speaking, and introduces students to culture typical of the
Dominican Republic.

Through completing the activities, students will employ critical
thinking skills as they compare the Spanish language and the culture
of the Dominician Republic with their own community. They will also
connect to other academic subjects, using their knowledge of Spanish
to access new information. In this unit, students are learning to talk
about sports, whom they know, what they know, parts of the body, and
staying healthy. In addition, they will learn to make excuses and say
what they did. They are also learning about grammar—the verb **jugar**
(to play), the verbs **saber** and **conocer** (to know), the personal **a,** the
verb **doler** (to hurt), the preterite of **-ar** verbs, and the preterite of **-car,
-gar, -zar** verbs.

Please feel free to call me with any questions or concerns you
might have as your student practices reading, writing, listening, and
speaking in Spanish.

Sincerely,

Family Involvement Activity

Put your imagination to work!

Hidden words

In this game players unscramble the English words for parts of the body, then write the Spanish equivalents for the English words.

1.	IKNS	
2.	MTCAHSO	
3.	OTMHU	
4.	REA	
5.	NADH	
6.	EKNAL	
7.	ENKE	
8.	DEHA	
9.	RAM	
10.	YBDO	
11.	ENSO	
12.	REHAT	

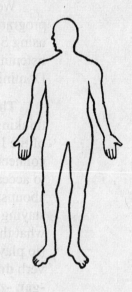

STEP 1

Make a copy of the scrambled words for each of the participants. Distribute the papers upside down so nobody can read them before you start the game.

STEP 2

When you give the signal, all participants should turn the papers over and start to unscramble the words. They should try to unscramble as many words as they can in five minutes and write the Spanish words next to them.

STEP 3

The answers are in Spanish in the table below. Check players' answers, giving one point for each word found.

Write everyone's scores on a piece of paper.

Answers:

1.	piel		**7.**	rodilla
2.	estómago		**8.**	cabeza
3.	boca		**9.**	brazo
4.	oído		**10.**	pie
5.	mano		**11.**	nariz
6.	tobillo		**12.**	corazón

UNIDAD 6

Family Involvement Activity

Absent Student Copymasters

Presentación / Práctica de vocabulario

Materials Checklist

- ☐ Student text
- ☐ DVD
- ☐ Video activities copymasters
- ☐ TXT CD 6 tracks 1–2
- ☐ L1B TXT CD 1 track 16
- ☐ *Cuaderno* pages 246–248 (L1B pp. 50–52)
- ☐ *Cuaderno para hispanohablantes* pages 246–249 (L1B pp. 50–53)
- ☐ Did You Get It? Copymasters 1–2, 10
- ☐ ClassZone.com

Steps to Follow

- ☐ Study the vocabulary of **Presentación de vocabulario** (L1 pp. 302–303, L1B pp. 104–106) by reading the words above the photos and the accompanying text. Watch the DVD and complete the video activities copymasters.
- ☐ Practice the words of the **Más vocabulario** box on page 302 (L1B p. 104). Read the words aloud. Write the words in your notebook.
- ☐ Listen to the CD as you read the vocabulary words again. Repeat the words after they are spoken.
- ☐ Listen to TXT CD 6 track 2, and complete the **¡A responder!** activity on page 303 (L1B p. 106; L1B TXT CD 1 track 16).
- ☐ Complete **Práctica de vocabulario** on page 304 (L1B p. 107), **Actividades 1** and **2**.
- ☐ Complete *Cuaderno* pages 246, 247, and 248 (L1B pp. 50–52).
  OR
  Complete *Cuaderno para hispanohablantes* pages 246, 247, 248, and 249 (L1B pp. 50–53).
- ☐ Complete Did You Get It? Copymasters 1, 2, and 10.
- ☐ Check your comprehension by completing the **Para y piensa** box on page 304 (L1B p. 107).

If You Don't Understand . . .

- ☐ Watch the DVD and listen to the CD in a quiet place. Imitate the voices of the actors on the recordings.
- ☐ Use the Interactive Flashcards to help you study the lesson.

Absent Student Copymasters

Vocabulario en contexto

Materials Checklist

☐ Student text

☐ DVD 2

☐ Video activities copymasters

☐ TXT CD 6 track 3

☐ Did You Get It? Copymasters 1, 3, 11

Steps to Follow

☐ Analyze the photo on page 305 (L1B p. 108).

☐ Read **Cuando lees** and **Cuando escuchas** on page 305 (L1B p. 108). Try to predict the answers to the questions.

☐ Watch the DVD for **Unidad 6, Telehistoria escena 1** without your book. Then watch the DVD again and complete the video activities copymasters.

☐ Listen to the CD for **Unidad 6, Telehistoria escena 1**. Follow along in the book as you listen. Try to understand the dialogue using the pictures and the context.

☐ Study the words in the **También se dice** box.

☐ Complete **Actividades 3** and **4** (L1 p. 306).

☐ Complete **Actividades 3** and **4** (L1B p. 109).

☐ Complete Did You Get It? Copymasters 1, 3, and 11.

☐ Check your comprehension by completing the **Para y piensa** box on page 306 (L1B p. 109).

If You Don't Understand . . .

☐ Be sure to watch the DVD and listen to the CD where you can focus completely. Pause and rewind if you don't understand a section.

☐ In **Actividad 4**, do the parts of both partners.

☐ Read aloud everything that you write. Be sure that you understand what you are reading.

☐ Make a list of questions for your teacher if anything is not clear.

☐ Say aloud the sentence you are thinking of writing before you begin to write. Read it aloud again after you write it.

Absent Student Copymasters

Presentación / Práctica de gramática

Materials Checklist

☐ Student text

☐ *Cuaderno* pages 249–251 (L1B pp. 53–55)

☐ *Cuaderno para hispanohablantes* pages 250–252 (L1B pp. 54–56)

☐ TXT CD 6 track 4

☐ L1B TXT CD 1 track 17

☐ Did You Get It? Copymasters 4, 5, 12

☐ ClassZone.com

Steps to Follow

☐ Read about the verb **jugar** on page 307. Conjugate the verb aloud several times.

☐ Complete **Actividades 5**, **6**, and **7** (L1 p. 308). Use TXT CD 6 track 4.

☐ Complete **Actividades 5**, **6**, and **7** (L1B p. 111). Use L1B TXT CD 1 track 17.

☐ Complete **Actividades 8** and **9** (L1 p. 309).

☐ Complete **Actividades 8** and **9** (L1B p. 112).

☐ Complete **Actividades 10** and **11** (L1B p. 113).

☐ Complete the *Cuaderno* pages 249, 250, and 251 (L1B pp. 53–55).
OR
Complete the *Cuaderno para hispanohablantes* pages 250, 251, and 252
(L1B pp. 54–56).

☐ Complete Did You Get It? Copymasters 4, 5, and 12.

☐ Check your comprehension by completing the **Para y piensa** box on page 309
(L1B p. 113).

If You Don't Understand . . .

☐ Conjugate the verb aloud while looking at the textbook chart. Practice making new sentences using the verb.

☐ Use the model sentences in the book as a guide for creating your own sentences.

☐ In the activities that require a partner, practice both parts of the dialogue.

☐ Use the Animated Grammar to help you understand.

☐ Use the Leveled Grammar Practice on the @Home Tutor.

Absent Student Copymasters

Gramática en contexto

Materials Checklist

- [ ] Student text
- [ ] DVD 2
- [ ] Video activities copymasters
- [ ] TXT CD 6 tracks 5–6
- [ ] Did You Get It? Copymasters 4, 6

Steps to Follow

- [ ] Look at the photo on page 310 (L1B p. 114) and predict what may be happening in the dialogue.

- [ ] Read **Cuando lees** and **Cuando escuchas** under *Strategies* on page 310 (L1B p. 114). Copy the questions.

- [ ] Read **Telehistoria escena 2**. Try to understand the dialogue.

- [ ] Watch the DVD for **Unidad 6**, **Telehistoria escena 2** without your book. Then watch the DVD again and complete the video activities copymasters.

- [ ] Listen to the CD for **Unidad 6**, **Telehistoria escena 2** and follow along in the book. Try to understand the dialogue using the pictures and the context.

- [ ] Study the words in the **También se dice** box.

- [ ] Complete **Actividades 10** and **11** on page 311. Complete the parts of both partners in **Actividad 11**.

- [ ] Complete **Actividades 12** and **13** (L1B p. 115).

- [ ] Listen to TXT CD 6 track 6 as you follow along in the **Pronunciación** activity on page 311 (L1B p. 115).

- [ ] Complete Did You Get It? Copymasters 4 and 6.

- [ ] Check your comprehension by completing the **Para y piensa** box on page 311.

If You Don't Understand . . .

- [ ] Use the DVD and the CD to help you understand the lesson. Pause the recordings and go back as often as you need.

- [ ] Listen to the CD for **Actividad 10** to help you with sentence structure and pronunciation.

- [ ] Reread **Unidad 6**, **Telehistoria escena 2** to know how to create your sentences correctly.

Absent Student Copymasters

Presentación / Práctica de gramática

Materials Checklist

- [ ] Student text
- [ ] *Cuaderno* pages 252–254 (L1B pp. 56–58)
- [ ] *Cuaderno para hispanohablantes* pages 253–256 (L1B pp. 57–60)
- [ ] Did You Get It? Copymasters 7–8
- [ ] ClassZone.com

Steps to Follow

- [ ] Study the verbs **saber** and **conocer** on page 312 (L1B p. 116).
- [ ] Do **Actividades 12** and **13** (L1 p. 313).
- [ ] Read the **Nota gramatical** box on page 313.
- [ ] Complete **Actividades 14** and **15** on page 314 (L1B p. 117).
- [ ] Complete **Actividades 16**, **17**, **18**, and **19** (L1B pp. 118–119).
- [ ] Complete the *Cuaderno* pages 252, 253, and 254 (L1B pp. 56–58).
  OR
  Complete the *Cuaderno para hispanohablantes* pages 253, 254, 255, and 256 (L1B pp. 57–60).
- [ ] Complete Did You Get It? Copymasters 7 and 8.
- [ ] Check your comprehension by completing the **Para y piensa** box on page 314 (L1B p. 119).

If You Don't Understand . . .

- [ ] Conjugate the verbs aloud while looking at the textbook chart. Practice making new sentences using that verb.
- [ ] Use the model sentences in the book as a guide for creating your own sentences.
- [ ] If you get confused, write down your questions for the teacher to answer later. Be as specific as possible.
- [ ] In the activities that require a partner, practice both parts of the dialogue.
- [ ] Check for meaning and correct spelling. Make sure you have included accent marks and other punctuation.
- [ ] Use the Animated Grammar to help you understand.
- [ ] Use the Leveled Grammar Practice on the @Home Tutor.

Absent Student Copymasters

UNIDAD 6 Lección 1

Absent Student Copymasters

Todo junto

Materials Checklist

☐ Student text

☐ Video activities copymasters

☐ *Cuaderno* pages 255–256 (L1B pp. 59–60)

☐ *Cuaderno para hispanohablantes* pages 257–258 (L1B pp. 61–62)

☐ TXT CD 6 tracks 7–9

☐ L1B TXT CD 1 tracks 18–19

☐ WB CD 3 tracks 21–24

☐ HL CD 2 tracks 9–12

☐ Did You Get It? Copymasters 7, 9

Steps to Follow

☐ Examine the photos on page 315 (L1B p. 120).

☐ Read **Cuando lees** and **Cuando escuchas** from *Strategies* on page 315 (L1B p. 120) and copy the questions.

☐ Read the **Resumen** of **escena 1** and **escena 2**. Read the script of **Telehistoria escena 3**.

☐ Listen to CD **Unidad 6** for **Telehistoria escena 3** and follow along in the book at the same time. Try to understand the dialogue using the pictures and the context.

☐ Watch the DVD for **Unidad 6**, **Telehistoria escena 3** without your book. Then watch the DVD again and complete the video activities copymasters.

☐ Complete **Actividades 16**, **17**, and **18** (L1 p. 316).

☐ Complete **Actividades 19** and **20** (L1 p. 317).

☐ Complete **Actividades 20**, **21**, **22**, **23**, and **24** (L1B pp. 121–122).

☐ Complete *Cuaderno* pages 255 and 256 (L1B pp. 59–60).
OR
Complete *Cuaderno para hispanohablantes* pages 257 and 258 (L1B pp. 61–62).

☐ Complete Did You Get It? Copymasters 7 and 9.

☐ Check your comprehension by completing the **Para y piensa** box on page 317 (L1B p. 122).

Absent Student Copymasters

Lectura y Conexiones

Materials Checklist

- ☐ Student text
- ☐ TXT CD 6 track 10

Steps to Follow

- ☐ Read **¡Avanza!** and **Strategy: Leer**, and follow the directions (L1 p. 318, L1B p. 124).

- ☐ Read the feature, **Un club de deportes** (L1 pp. 318–319, L1B pp. 124–125).

- ☐ Follow along with the text on TXT CD 6 track 10.

- ☐ Check your comprehension by completing the **¿Comprendiste?** and **¿Y tú?** sections of **Para y piensa** box on page 319 (L1B p. 125).

- ☐ Read **La bandera dominicana** on page 320 (L1B p. 126).

- ☐ Read **Proyecto 1, La historia**. Do the research for the activity.

- ☐ Design a flag for **Proyecto 2, El arte**.

- ☐ Read **La educación física** in **Proyecto 3**. Try to answer the question.

If You Don't Understand . . .

- ☐ Listen to the CD in a comfortable, quiet place. Pause and go back as often as necessary to keep up with the text.

- ☐ Read the selection carefully. Use the pictures to help you follow the text.

- ☐ If you have any questions, write them down so you can ask your teacher later.

- ☐ Think about your answers before you begin to write. Think about different ways to state your answer, and choose the best one.

- ☐ After you write your sentence, check to make sure that it says what you wanted to say.

Absent Student Copymasters

Repaso de la lección

Materials Checklist

- [ ] Student text
- [ ] *Cuaderno* pages 257–268 (L1B pp. 61–72)
- [ ] *Cuaderno para hispanohablantes* pages 259–268 (L1B pp. 63–72)
- [ ] TXT CD 6 track 11
- [ ] L1B TXT CD 1 track 20
- [ ] WB CD 3 tracks 25–30

Steps to Follow

- [ ] Read the bullet points under **¡Llegada!** on page 322 (L1B p. 128).
- [ ] Complete **Actividades 1**, **2**, **3**, **4**, and **5** (L1 pp. 322–323, L1B pp. 128–129).
- [ ] Complete *Cuaderno* pages 257, 258, and 259 (L1B pp. 61–63).
- [ ] Complete *Cuaderno* pages 260, 261, and 262 (L1B pp. 64–66).
  OR
  Complete *Cuaderno para hispanohablantes* pages 259, 260, 261, and 262 (L1B pp. 63–66).
- [ ] Complete *Cuaderno* pages 263, 264, and 265 (L1B pp. 67–69).
  OR
  Complete *Cuaderno para hispanohablantes* pages 263, 264, and 265 (L1B pp. 67–69).
- [ ] Complete *Cuaderno* pages 266, 267, and 268 (L1B pp. 70–72).
  OR
  Complete *Cuaderno para hispanohablantes* pages 266, 267, and 268 (L1B pp. 70–72).

If You Don't Understand . . .

- [ ] Read the activity directions several times.
- [ ] For activities that require the CD, listen to the CD in a quiet place. If you get lost, pause the CD and go back.
- [ ] Read the models to help you understand how to complete each activity.
- [ ] Think about what you would like to say before you write your answers. Read them to check for accuracy.
- [ ] Keep a list of questions for your teacher to answer later.

Absent Student Copymasters

Presentación / Práctica de vocabulario

Materials Checklist

- [ ] Student text
- [ ] DVD 2
- [ ] Video activities copymasters
- [ ] TXT CD 6 tracks 12–13
- [ ] LIB TXT CD 1 track 21
- [ ] *Cuaderno* pages 269–271 (L1B pp. 73–75)
- [ ] *Cuaderno para hispanohablantes* pages 269–272 (L1B pp. 73–76)
- [ ] Did You Get It? Copymasters 13–14
- [ ] ClassZone.com

Steps to Follow

- [ ] Study the new vocabulary in **Presentación de vocabulario** (L1 pp. 326–327, L1B pp. 132–134) by reading the captions of the photos. Watch the DVD and complete the video activities copymasters.

- [ ] Practice the words in the **Más vocabulario** box on page 326 (L1B p. 134). Read the words aloud. Write the words in your notebook.

- [ ] Listen to the CD and repeat the words aloud as you read the vocabulary words again.

- [ ] Listen to TXT CD 6 track 13, and complete the **¡A responder!** activity on page 327 (L1B p. 134; LIB TXT CD 1 track 21).

- [ ] Do **Práctica de vocabulario** (L1 p. 328, L1B p. 135). Complete **Actividades 1** and **2**.

- [ ] Complete *Cuaderno* pages 269, 270, and 271 (L1B pp. 73–75).
  OR
  Complete *Cuaderno para hispanohablantes* pages 269, 270, 271, and 272 (L1B pp. 73–76).

- [ ] Check your comprehension by completing the **Para y piensa** box on page 328 (L1B p. 135).

- [ ] Complete Did You Get It? Copymasters 13 and 14.

If You Don't Understand . . .

- [ ] Watch the DVD and listen to the CD in a quiet place. Imitate the voices of the actors on the recordings.

- [ ] Use the Interactive Flashcards to help you study the lesson.

Absent Student Copymasters

Vocabulario en contexto

Materials Checklist

- [ ] Student text
- [ ] DVD 2
- [ ] Video activities copymasters
- [ ] TXT CD 6 track 14
- [ ] Did You Get It? Copymasters 13, 15, 22, 23

Steps to Follow

- [ ] Look at the photos on page 329 (L1B 136).
- [ ] Read **Cuando lees** and **Cuando escuchas** on page 329 (L1B 136). Try to predict the answers to the questions.
- [ ] Listen to **Telehistoria escena 1** on TXT CD 6 track 14. Follow along in the book as you listen. Try to understand the dialogue using the pictures and the context.
- [ ] Watch the DVD for **Unidad 6**, **Telehistoria escena 1** without your book. Then watch the DVD again and and complete the video activities copymasters.
- [ ] Study the words in the **También se dice** box.
- [ ] Read **Nota gramatical** and complete **Actividades 3** and **4** on page 330 (L1B 137).
- [ ] Check your comprehension by completing the **Para y piensa** box on page 330 (L1B 137).
- [ ] Complete Did You Get It? Copymasters 13, 15, 22, and 23.

If You Don't Understand . . .

- [ ] Be sure to watch the DVD and listen to the CD where you can completely focus. Stop and play them again if you do not understand.
- [ ] Use the CD to help you understand **Actividad 3**.
- [ ] In **Actividad 4**, do the parts of both partners.
- [ ] Read aloud everything that you write. Be sure that you understand what you are reading.
- [ ] Make a list of questions for your teacher if anything is not clear.
- [ ] Say aloud the sentence you are thinking of writing before you begin to write.

Absent Student Copymasters

Level 1 pp. 331–333
Level 1B pp. 138–141

Presentación / Práctica de gramática

Materials Checklist

☐ Student text

☐ *Cuaderno* pages 272–274 (L1B pp. 76–78)

☐ *Cuaderno para hispanohablantes* pages 273–275 (L1B pp. 77–79)

☐ Did You Get It? Copymasters 16, 17, 24

☐ ClassZone.com

Steps to Follow

☐ Read about the preterite form of –**ar** verbs on page 331 (L1B 138). Conjugate the verbs aloud several times.

☐ Complete **Actividades 5** and **6** (L1 p. 332, L1B p. 139).

☐ Complete **Actividades 7** and **8** (L1 p. 333, L1B pp. 139–140).

☐ Do **Actividades 9** and **10** (L1B pp. 140–141).

☐ Complete the *Cuaderno* pages 272, 273, and 274 (L1B pp. 76–78).
OR
Complete the *Cuaderno para hispanohablantes* pages 273, 274, and 275 (L1B pp. 77–79).

☐ Check your comprehension by completing the **Para y piensa** box on page 333 (L1B p. 141).

☐ Complete Did You Get It? Copymasters 16, 17, and 24.

If You Don't Understand . . .

☐ Conjugate the verbs aloud while looking at the textbook chart. Practice making new sentences using each verb.

☐ In the activities that require a partner, practice both parts of the dialogue.

☐ Check for meaning and correct spelling. Make sure you have included accent marks and other punctuation.

☐ Use the Animated Grammar to help you understand.

☐ Use the Leveled Grammar Practice on the @Home Tutor.

Absent Student Copymasters

UNIDAD 6 Lección 2

Absent Student Copymasters

Gramática en contexto

Materials Checklist

- [ ] Student text
- [ ] DVD 2
- [ ] Video activities copymasters
- [ ] TXT CD 6 track 15
- [ ] Did You Get It? Copymasters 16, 18

Steps to Follow

- [ ] Examine the photo on page 334 (L1B p. 142) and predict what may be happening in this **Telehistoria**.

- [ ] Read **Cuando lees** and **Cuando escuchas** under *Strategies* on page 334 (L1B p. 142) and write the questions in your notebook.

- [ ] Read **Telehistoria escena 2**. Think about the comprehension questions.

- [ ] Listen to TXT CD 6 track 15 for **Telehistoria escena 2** as you follow along in the book. Try to understand the dialogue using the pictures and the context.

- [ ] Watch the DVD for **Unidad 6**, **Telehistoria escena 2** without your book. Then watch the DVD again and complete the video activities copymasters.

- [ ] Complete **Actividades 9**, **10**, and **11** (L1 p. 335).

- [ ] Complete **Actividades 11**, **12**, and **13** (L1B p. 143).

- [ ] Check your comprehension by completing the **Para y piensa** box on page 335 (L1B p. 143).

- [ ] Complete Did You Get It? Copymasters 16 and 18.

If You Don't Understand . . .

- [ ] Use the DVD and the CD to help you understand the lesson. Play the recordings as often as you need.

- [ ] Listen to the CD for **Actividad 9** to help you with sentence structure and pronunciation.

- [ ] Reread **Escena 2** and other examples in the text if you need help with your sentence structure.

- [ ] Read aloud everything that you write to see if you wrote what you intended to say.

Absent Student Copymasters

Presentación / Práctica de gramática

Materials Checklist

☐ Student text

☐ *Cuaderno* pages 275–277 (L1B pp. 79–81)

☐ *Cuaderno para hispanohablantes* pages 276–279 (L1B pp. 80–83)

☐ TXT CD 6 tracks 16–17

☐ L1B TXT CD 1 track 22

☐ Did You Get It? Copymasters 19, 20

☐ ClassZone.com

Steps to Follow

☐ Study the preterite form of verbs ending in **–car**, **–gar**, and **–zar** on page 336 (L1B p. 144). Conjugate the verbs aloud several times.

☐ Do **Actividades 12** and **13** on page 337. Use TXT CD 6 track 16 to complete **Actividad 13**.

☐ Read the **Pronunciación** box on page 337 (L1B p. 146). Use TXT CD 6 track 17 with the activity.

☐ Complete **Actividades 14** and **15** (L1 p. 338, L1B p. 145).

☐ Complete **Actividades 16**, **17**, **18**, and **19** (L1B pp. 146–147). Use L1B TXT CD 1 track 22 for **Actividad 16**.

☐ Complete the *Cuaderno* pages 275, 276, and 277 (L1B pp. 79–81).
OR
Complete the *Cuaderno para hispanohablantes* pages 276, 277, 278, and 279 (L1B pp. 80–83).

☐ Check your comprehension by completing the **Para y piensa** box on page 338 (L1B p. 147).

☐ Complete Did You Get It? Copymasters 19 and 20.

If You Don't Understand . . .

☐ In the activities that have parts for two people, practice both parts of the dialogue.

☐ Check for meaning and correct spelling. Make sure you have included accent marks and other punctuation.

☐ Use the Animated Grammar to help you understand.

☐ Use the Leveled Grammar Practice on the @Home Tutor.

Absent Student Copymasters

Todo junto

Materials Checklist

☐ Student text

☐ DVD 2

☐ Video activities copymasters

☐ *Cuaderno* pages 278–279 (L1B pp. 82–83)

☐ *Cuaderno para hispanohablantes* pages 280–281 (L1B pp. 84–85)

☐ TXT CD 6 tracks 18–20

☐ L1B TXT CD 1 tracks 23–24

☐ WB CD 3 tracks 31–34

☐ HL CD 2 tracks 13–16

☐ Did You Get It? Copymasters 19, 21

Steps to Follow

☐ Read **Cuando lees** and **Cuando escuchas** from *Strategies* on page 339 (L1B p. 148) and copy the questions.

☐ Read the **Resumen** of **Escena 1** and **Escena 2** on page 339 (L1B p. 148). Read the script of **Escena 3**.

☐ Listen to TXT CD 6 track 18 for **Telehistoria escena 3** as you follow along in the book. Try to understand the dialogue using the pictures and the context.

☐ Watch the DVD for **Unidad 6**, **Telehistoria escena 3** without your book. Then watch the DVD again and complete the video activities copymasters.

☐ Complete **Actividades 16**, **17**, **18**, **19**, and **20** on pages 340 and 341.

☐ Complete **Actividades 20**, **21**, **22**, **23**, and **24** (L1B pp. 149–150).

☐ Complete *Cuaderno* pages 278 and 279 (L1B pp. 82–83).
OR
Complete *Cuaderno para hispanohablantes* pages 280 and 281 (L1B pp. 84–85).

☐ Check your comprehension by completing the **Para y piensa** box on page 341 (L1B p. 150).

☐ Complete Did You Get It? Copymasters 19 and 21.

Absent Student Copymasters

Lectura cultural

Materials Checklist

- [ ] Student text
- [ ] TXT CD 6 track 21

Steps to Follow

- [ ] Read the **Strategy: Leer** (L1 p. 342, L1B p. 152).

- [ ] Read **¡Avanza!** and **Dos atletas de alta velocidad** on pages 342 and 343 (L1B pp. 152–153).

- [ ] Follow along with the text on TXT CD 6 track 21.

- [ ] Check your comprehension by completing the **¿Comprendiste?** and **¿Y tú?** sections of the **Para y piensa** box on page 343 (L1B p. 153).

If You Don't Understand . . .

- [ ] Listen to the CD in a quiet place. Pause and go back as often as you need. Imitate the voices of the people on the recording.

- [ ] Read the questions and your answers out loud.

- [ ] If you have any questions, make a list so you can ask your teacher later.

- [ ] Think about what you are trying to say before you write your answer. Make sure it makes sense to you and experiment with different ways of saying your sentence.

Absent Student Copymasters

Proyectos culturales

Materials Checklist

☐ Student text

Steps to Follow

☐ Read **Gestos y refranes** and look at the illustrations (L1 p. 344, L1B p. 154).

☐ Follow the instructions to complete **Los Gestos** in **Proyecto 1**.

☐ Follow the instructions to do **Proyecto 2**, **Los Refranes**.

☐ Read the **En tu comunidad** segment and write your answer in your notebook.

If You Don't Understand . . .

☐ Read the activity directions a few times, silently and then aloud.

☐ Practice the parts of both partners in **Proyecto 1**.

☐ If you have any doubts or observations, write them down so you can discuss them with your teacher later.

☐ Think about what you want to say before you begin writing. Think of several ways to say it, then choose the best one.

Absent Student Copymasters

Repaso de la lección

Materials Checklist

☐ Student text

☐ *Cuaderno* pages 280–291 (L1B pp. 84–95)

☐ *Cuaderno para hispanohablantes* pages 282–291 (L1B pp. 86–95)

☐ TXT CD 6 track 22

☐ LIB TXT CD 1 track 25

☐ WB CD 3 tracks 35–40

Steps to Follow

☐ Read the bullet points under **¡Llegada!** on page 346 (L1B p. 156).

☐ Complete **Actividades 1**, **2**, **3**, **4**, and **5** (L1 pp. 346–347, L1B pp. 156–157).

☐ Complete *Cuaderno* pages 280, 281, and 282 (L1B pp. 84–86).

☐ Complete *Cuaderno* pages 283, 284, and 285 (L1B pp. 87–89).
OR
Complete *Cuaderno para hispanohablantes* pages 282, 283, 284, and 285
(L1B pp. 86–89).

☐ Complete *Cuaderno* pages 286, 287, and 288 (L1B pp. 90–92).
OR
Complete *Cuaderno para hispanohablantes* pages 286, 287, and 288
(L1B pp. 90–92).

☐ Complete *Cuaderno* pages 289, 290, and 291 (L1B pp. 93–95).
OR
Complete *Cuaderno para hispanohablantes* pages 289, 290, and 291
(L1B pp. 93–95).

If You Don't Understand . . .

☐ Read the activity directions several times. Say them out loud.

☐ For **Actividad 1**, listen to the CD in a quiet place. If you get lost, pause the CD and go back.

☐ Read the models silently and aloud to help you understand how to complete each activity.

☐ Think about what you would like to say before you write your answers. Read them to check for accuracy.

☐ Keep a list of questions for your teacher to answer later.

Absent Student Copymasters

Comparación cultural

Materials Checklist

- [ ] Student text
- [ ] TXT CD 6 track 23

Steps to Follow

- [ ] Read the directions in **Lectura y escritura** for **Actividades 1** and **2** on page 348 (L1B 158).

- [ ] Listen to TXT CD 6 track 23 as you read **Deportes favoritos** on page 349 (L1B 159).

- [ ] Read **Strategy: Escribir**, then begin **Actividad 2** (L1 p. 348, L1B 158).

- [ ] Complete the **Compara con tu mundo** section on page 348 (L1B 158).

If You Don't Understand . . .

- [ ] Read through all of the instructions before you begin reading the feature.

- [ ] Listen to the CD in a quiet place. Pause and go back as often as necessary.

- [ ] Look up words you don't know.

- [ ] Make a list of questions if you are confused or don't know how to say something. Think of what you do know how to say.

- [ ] Think about what you want to say before you begin writing. Read everything you write to make sure it is clear.

Absent Student Copymasters

Repaso inclusivo

Materials Checklist

- [ ] Student text
- [ ] TXT CD 6 track 24

Steps to Follow

- [ ] Use TXT CD 6 track 24 to complete **Actividad 1** on page 350 (L1B p. 160). Imitate the pronunciation of the voices on the CD.

- [ ] Complete **Actividades 2**, **3**, **4**, **5**, **6**, and **7** (L1 pp. 350–351, L1B pp. 160–161).

If You Don't Understand . . .

- [ ] For **Actividad 1**, listen to the CD in a quiet place. If you get lost, pause the CD and go back.

- [ ] Read the activity directions several times. Use the textbook and review the vocabulary and verb conjugations you need to complete each activity.

- [ ] Write and practice the parts of both partners in all activities that call for partner work.

- [ ] Think about what you want to say before you begin to write. Read aloud everything that you write. Make sure that it makes sense.

- [ ] If you have any questions, write them down for your teacher to answer later.